modernism and
modernization in
architecture

edited by **Helen Castle**

modernism and

modernization in

architecture

A.R ACADEMY EDITIONS

First published in Great Britain in 1999 by Academy Editions

A division of
JOHN WILEY & SONS Ltd
Baffins Lane
Chichester
West Sussex PO19 1UD

ISBN 0-471-98469-8

Other Wiley editorial offices
New York • Weinheim • Brisbane • Singapore • Toronto

Designed by Mark Vernon-Jones

Printed and bound in Italy

Acknowledgements My thanks must go firstly to Maggie Toy for her endless enthusiasm and for having an adventurous spirit, giving me the chance to carry through this project; to Ellie Duffy for her enduring faith and encouragement, and her talents in co-ordination; to Mark Vernon-Jones whose creative vision has transformed text and pictures into a beautiful book; and to Christine Davis for her unstinting rigour.

All the contributors to this book gave more of their time and knowledge than we could pay them for. Botond Bognar, Iain Borden, Ilse Crawford, Jayne Merkel, Jeremy Myerson and Antoine Predock have all displayed exceptional generosity. Thanks to Jayne Merkel, in particular, who has has taught me much about New York architecture and life in the course of our e-mail correspondence. Thanks must also be offered to those who gave statements, project descriptions and pictures.

I would also like to offer my personal thanks to Craig and Rosa for their patience; and to my Mum and Dad and Jill who looked after Rosa so well when I was working on the project; and to Wendy Hitchmough for being such a good professional friend.

Frontispiece: Antoine Predock,
Turtle Creek House, Dallas,
Texas, 1993

For **Craig** and **Rosa**

contents

Deciding whether to give the word 'modernism'
an upper or lower case 'm' is now a prerequisite
to writing about the modern.' Many of the buildings featured
in this book probably justify a capital 'm',
being immediately recognizable as 'Modernist' in style, whether they
adopt the sharp white forms of the 1930s Modern Movement
or the freer, more frivolous Pop-influenced designs of the 1960s.
It is not, however, their formal qualities alone that make them particularly 'modern', or interesting; a building that echoes the International Style of the 1930s or 1940s can now be regarded as pastiche, or even historical revivalism. In the 1990s, modern architecture has distinguished itself from its modernist predecessors by being part of a broader cultural movement. In the first half of the twentieth century modernism was largely confined to the arts – music, literature, fine art and design – whereas now it can be perceived in many more aspects of contemporary life, from restaurant and furniture design to the media and politics. Today's 'modern movement' can be characterized by its desire to pursue the progressive and the innovative, by its urge to modernize and rationalize, whatever discipline is involved – whether it be in tackling legislation, or in styling an interior.

The sense that architecture should only be looked at in terms of a larger picture, made the inclusion of voices from other disciplines a necessity in this book. By featuring statements from various individuals and institutions that have been central to this movement, the opening section is intended to demonstrate just how ubiquitous and penetrating it has been.

In Britain, the recognition of the importance of a modern approach has been particularly marked in politics. After seventeen years of Conservative rule, this can only be attributed to the general *zeitgeist*, which has manifested itself in an overwhelming enthusiasm for all things new. As Ilse Crawford, founding editor of British *Elle Decoration*, has written: 'The government has changed, a class-conscious aesthetic is no longer appropriate; modern equals optimism and looking-forward.'[2] This zest for innovation has been encapsulated by the Labour government's determination to modernize institutions and legislation. Since the 1997 British general election, 'modernization' has become an all too common soundbite, tripped off the tongue of the Labour Prime Minister Tony Blair and even echoed by the Leader of the Opposition William Hague. When Blair hosted the 'sofa summit' at Canary Wharf in November 1997 and treated the French president and his prime minister to a European-style lunch

Introduction   *Helen Castle*

seated on sofas designed by a protégé of Sir Terence Conran, Jacques Chirac rewarded Blair with a compliment that was right on cue, describing him as '*jeune, dynamique et moderne*'.[3]

It is not, however, only in politics that the new British government has emphasized the importance of an innovating force. In April 1998, the Department of Trade and Industry staged 'powerhouse::uk', an exhibition housed in a silver-domed space designed by Nigel Coates for a site behind Horse Guards Parade, just round the corner from Downing Street. The express intention was to promote modern British creativity to an 'influential and international audience' of delegates attending the London Asian European Summit. It was, perhaps, the first time that a British government had so outwardly, in the heart of Whitehall, promoted modern design and technology and recognized its potential for commerce and industry. In his statement (page 16), John Battle MP, Minister of State for Science, Energy and Industry, demonstrates the degree to which government policy has come to consider British modern design and creative thinking a highly saleable export (the British press have coined the phrase 'Cool Britannia' to describe the phenomenon). For Battle, the link between business and creativity is inextricable: 'This Government is committed to Britain leading the way into the next millennium as a creative and forward-thinking nation with whom it is good to do business.'

It is not only new voices who have been important in establishing modernism as a force in the 1990s. Individuals such as Sir Terence Conran and Lord Rogers, who began their careers in the 1960s, have never ceased to advocate viable modern design. They withstood the anti-modern sentiments of the 1970s and 1980s to become establishment figures – now even recognized with knighthoods. In his statement (page 21), Richard Rogers emphasizes the importance for contemporary design of an inclusive notion of modernism, which goes beyond the purism of the early twentieth-century International Style. For him, evolution is as necessary a process as is his search for 'a more open and yet harmonious order'. As a restaurateur, furniture designer and entrepreneur, Terence Conran has probably been one of the most influential figures in popularizing the modern. His restaurants have injected a sophistication never previously experienced in London (see Mezzo, page 37), both in terms of their food and their interiors. It is perhaps his advocacy of a sensual and practical strain of modernism, which can so easily be applied to the domestic, that has made his various enterprises so successful: 'Architecture and design – when they relate to our homes in particular – must accommodate human, everyday needs. Modernism, I believe, reconciles simplicity with the emotional, spiritual and physical aspects of comfort' (see page 18).

Previous page Tom Dixon, Jacks, 1997. These stacking seats are part of a range of highly coloured, Pop-inspired furniture, which includes Stars, Knobs, Tubs and Melons. **Right** Branson Coates, 'powerhouse::uk', Horse Guards Parade, London, April 1998. This temporary exhibition space displayed British creativity in its four separate domes, themed as 'lifestyle', 'communication', 'networking' and 'learning'. **Opposite** 'High Cool', *Wallpaper**, January/February 1997. Here Berthold Lubetkin's 1930s architecture is celebrated by a photo shoot that features contemporary designer fashion and furniture.

One of the most important influences on modernism in the 1990s has been the media, and most significantly the interiors magazines. This is particularly the case in Britain, where they have been central in changing perceptions of what to be 'modern' is. Whereas the disciples of the Modern Movement were typically earnest and sincere in their social and political aims, today's modernists are projected as hip, urban and young with plenty of disposable income to spend. As the interiors writer Fiona Murphy puts it: 'In the 1990s those who live in clean architectural spaces are presented as the tousle-headed young – not campaigners, just hedonists'.[4] Whereas in the early 1980s British interiors magazines such as *World of Interiors* and *House and Garden* were the preserve of home counties' housewives, *Elle Decoration* (launched in 1989) and *Wallpaper** (first issued September/October 1996) broke away from the realm of frilly country houses and ruched curtains by being self-consciously modern and establishing for themselves a younger readership.[5] If *Elle Decoration* blazed the way, *Wallpaper** has pioneered a new approach to publishing architecture and interiors. Modern architect-designed spaces have become a backdrop to the designer clothes that people wear and the objects they covet. A *Wallpaper** fashion shoot in which the models lounged around on Eames and Saarinen chairs, for instance, was set in Berthold Lubetkin's penthouse at Highpoint in north London. The editorial enthused over the flat as if it were an essential new fashion accessory: 'Gaining access to shoot Highpoint's penthouse was something of a coup for our interiors team. "Once we saw it we knew we had to have it," explains design editor Toni Spencer. "It's just so sexy."'[6] Founding editor Tyler Brûlé has more than fulfilled his promise at the title's launch to deliver 'an indulgent magazine for men and women, covering interiors, architecture, entertaining and travel, which will be consumed by all things contemporary' (see page 17).

The vision of the modern that Ilse Crawford has in the last few years developed at *Elle Decoration* is quite distinct from that of *Wallpaper**. Whereas interiors, in Tyler Brûlé's view, fuse with a greater cosmopolitan and metropolitan culture to become 'the stuff

that surrounds you', Crawford sees them in terms of a modernized notion of 'home', as the 'pleasure zone' that provides a necessary haven from the stresses of contemporary life. Following from this, her take on 'the modern' is one that is softer, more comfortable and more feminine than the sort of mid-twentieth-century corporate American style that *Wallpaper** often espouses. Above all, it is sensual.

Although a more indulgent and seductive image of modernism has sold 'the modern' to a wider audience, its viability as an aesthetic is dependent on its successful adaptation by high-street retailers; after all, the items featured in magazines tend to be those that people aspire to rather than those they are actually able to buy. In Britain, the Swedish company IKEA has almost single-handedly been responsible for converting the British to 'good modern affordable design' (see page 20). Their superstores persuasively sell every conceivable household item, from a garlic crusher to a double bed. IKEA's success can be attributed to both the cheapness of the goods on sale and the overall shopping experience that it cultivates. Located on main roads out of town, the stores are complete environments in themselves. The theme-park atmosphere allows the shopper to relax into a sense that they are having a day out, doing something other than purchasing items for their home: the showrooms are laid out as a 'yellow brick road' trail that passes through a multicoloured ball-filled crèche, Swedish-style restaurant, various room sets and 'the marketplace', where smaller items are displayed. Among their various lines can be found approximations of Alvar Aalto's bentwood furniture, Arne Jacobsen chairs and the Eames' DCM chair.

Having established the ubiquity of modernism, the statements open up the way for a more critical examination of the subject. For this title's *raison d'être* is to initiate a discussion of modernism that is particular to its condition in the 1990s. This is the intention of the three essays poised at the beginning of the main body of the book that deal with the politics of modernism, its essential spirit and its manifestation in architecture, respectively. Although much has been written about the Modern Movement in the first half of the twentieth century, little of it has any bearing on modernism today. Some new modernism may depend on the International Style for its outward appearance, but its character greatly diverges from that of its aesthetic antecedents. For whereas the modernism of the first half of this century, at least in Europe, largely represented a critique of mainstream materialistic society, the modern today embraces commercialism and is used largely as an image through which to sell consumer products. When Aalto's Savoy vase was first manufactured in 1937, for instance, it used cheap bottle glass blown in moulds in an attempt to produce 'functional wares that were to be affordable for all but the very poorest'.[7] In 1998, these same vases were on sale at MoMA (the Museum of Modern Art) Design Store in New York. This shop, which is dedicated to the sale of 'modern design classics', sells goods that have been 'chosen for successfully integrating function with clean, modern lines and appropriate materials,' and which 'serve virtually all aspects of life in the 1990s'.[8]

Ironically enough, the all-pervasive consumerism of the 1990s probably delivers 'modern' objects to a wider customer base than was the case in the 1930s, when designers and manufacturers were first setting out to deliver tasteful and functional wares to the masses. Many critical writings on consumption and culture are therefore now out of kilter with the times. For much of the opposition to consumerism in the 1980s was a product, in Britain at least, of the polarization of politics brought about by the Conservatives' dismantling of the welfare state. Such opposition was a sort of desperate swansong for the postwar vision of, if not a socialist society, at least a more egalitarian one. Being backward-looking, this stance had little ultimately to offer present or future society. As cultural critic Raymond Williams wrote in 1985 of some of his contemporaries: 'Some of the best people of our time speak now only in this dark language. Their grave voices have to compete with the jingles of happy consumption, the only widespread form of contemporary optimism.'[9]

The general acknowledgement that opposition to a consumer society is no longer viable, or appropriate, thus places critical discussions of modernism at an impasse, begging the question: How is it possible to move forwards from here? Iain Borden's essay, 'Resurrection Politics' (pages 22–9), is an attempt to provide an answer. Borden looks beyond 'the old model of the welfare state, of organized provision' to a politics of modernism that recognizes that we are at 'the beginning of the fragmented state of consumption'. It is a project in which the authority of the state is replaced by 'the joint venture between self, society, company, institution and government'. It is a 'politics of difference' in which the 'experience of the modern' replaces an earlier emphasis on modernity. In architecture, this new model enables people to become empowered by being the subjects, rather than mere users, and inhabitants of buildings.

In 'All Modern and Emotional' (pages 30–5), Ilse Crawford places a barometer to the spirit of the times. She looks to social changes to explain how modernism has been tailored to the needs of the 1990s. To Crawford, modernism has for many people become a means through which

Opposite RAA Chair, IKEA, 1997. The influence of Charles and Ray Eames' moulded plywood DCM Chair of 1946 is evident in this design. **Above** Winter 1997 catalogue for the MoMA Design Store, New York. The cover shows the Butterfly Stool, designed by Sori Yanagi in 1956 and stocked by the store. **Right** Alvar Aalto, Blue Vase. First designed by Aalto during the 1930s, the famous Savoy vases were part of the merchandise available during the 1998 MoMA exhibition celebrating the centenary of Aalto's birth.

their fast-changing working patterns and lives are expressed. Above all else, she locates these changes in the shift towards female values. This feminization of modernism gives 'a more tolerant and hedonistic spin on the modern – it is sensual and emotional rather than rational and cutting edge'.

In the 1990s, the restaurant, the ultimate site of consumption, has come to offer a wider public a new and positive experience of the modern. This is particularly the case in London where people's contact with new design has hitherto been limited: suburban homes have traditionally been conventionally furnished and are generally imitative of a historical style, while offices as a rule are utilitarian and sterile. The contemporary interiors of London restaurants have in themselves become an attraction, giving people not only the possibility of enjoying 'happening' surroundings but also the opportunity to participate in an ambience of noisy bustle during the course of their meal. In his essay on London restaurants (pages 36–41), Jeremy Myerson explores this phenomenon by looking at three large-scale eateries and their handling of architectural space. He particularly focuses on the idea of 'light and air' and the way it is most often employed to modernist effect.

The body of the book is divided up into geographical regions: Britain, the USA (New York and the West) and Japan. Each region comprises an introductory essay and selected project descriptions. This is not an attempt at a survey of contemporary modernism, but aims rather to give an account of its diversity and its separate histories within each given area. British modernism, for instance, is seen in relief against the tide of anti-modernist sentiment in the 1980s and in the context of the high-tech architects who continued to champion modern design throughout this period. The works featured, however, are those which have shown not only an allegiance to modern design but also to a modernizing tendency. Fin and Future Systems are included for their emphasis on innovative technologies and processes, as well as their futuristic leanings, while three houses by Mark Guard have been selected to show the way he experiments with the domestic plan to create houses that attempt to meet contemporary needs in their layouts. Seth Stein's Pied-à-terre in Knightsbridge is a beautiful and finely detailed house, with its own quirky modern character. It was designed to tackle thoroughly typical current urban conditions: a tiny site with very restricted planning controls.

The US, 'the oldest modern country in the world', according to Gertrude Stein, has been subdivided into two sections.[10] In 'Modernism Redux' (pages 64–77), Jayne Merkel gives an account of modern architecture in the USA's cultural capital, taking it full circle from Philip Goodwin and Edward Durrell Stone's 1939 galleries for MoMA to Yoshio Taniguchi's 1997–8 planned scheme to renovate and expand the museum. Merkel shows how the notion of modernism in New York is embedded in the ideas set down in HR Hitchcock and Philip Johnson's seminal book *The International Style: Architecture Since 1922*, in which 'the modern' was conceived as a style rather than a social movement 'associated with modern art, European influence and cultural elite'. Modernism in the 1990s, however, represents a cultural journey through the post-modernism of the 1970s and 1980s, which has finally brought it to 'a de-radicalized, aestheticized, late twentieth-century form of modernism that respects historic architecture and absorbs it, instead of rejecting its premises and charting a completely new course.'

In her choice of projects, Jayne Merkel emphasizes this 'quieter', 'absorptive' mode of the 1990s. She includes two galleries by Richard Gluckman, one of the first architects of the late 1980s to work in a reductive manner. In the Dia Art Foundation of 1987, Gluckman used the minimalist artworks displayed in the gallery to find a new architectural language. The Paula Cooper Gallery, designed almost a decade later, develops this aesthetic further. The projects by Richard Meier and Bernard Tschumi – the Offices of Richard Meier & Partners and 17th Street Residential Loft, respectively – are two important instances of architects working in an uncharacteristically minimalist manner for themselves within a New York context in the late 1980s. Yoshio Taniguchi's design for the extension and renovation of MoMA – the most restrained entry in the museum's competition – exemplifies how this spirit of modern repose has prevailed at the end of the 1990s. At the beginning of the decade, however, this was not a foregone conclusion. Working in a sensitive historical setting at Pierpont Morgan Library, Bartholomew Voorsanger's Garden Court of 1990 broke new ground with its successful adoption of a modern design. The court is a contemporary palimpsest to McKim, Mead & White's original library. Merkel's final selection – Pasanella + Klein Stolzman + Berg's Williamsburg Community Center in Brooklyn – stands in contrast to the other projects she discusses. While these are primarily a product of the downtown and culturally self-conscious metropolis, the Brooklyn project is situated in the context of an International Style-type housing scheme and is composed of industrial materials and imagery.

If the treatment of modern architecture in New York can be traced back to ideas imported from Europe in the 1930s, the work carried out in the western US can be regarded as having an even older genesis. In 'Empathy versus Ideas' (pages 92–5), Antoine Predock, the internationally renowned architect whose practice is based in Albuquerque, New Mexico, attributes the emphasis placed on site-specificity in the west to the inescapable and commanding presence of prehistoric

Opposite Charles and Ray Eames, Plywood Lounge Chair, 1946. Although the popularity of Eames' furniture today means that original designs are still in production with Herman Miller and Vitra, original pieces have become collectors' items. The clamour for modern classics is such that the market has even penetrated the Internet, with a specialist in Eames, Graham Mancha, setting up an online service selling furniture and accessories (www.mancha.demon.co.uk).

American Indian sites and the 'vast landscape with its ineffable space'. It is a 'homegrown' modernist tradition which has its roots in the architecture of Frank Lloyd Wright and Louis Kahn, whose work responded to the uniquely American environment and its scenery. This approach is illustrated by two of Predock's own projects, Turtle Creek House and the Spencer Theater. Commissioned by a couple who are keen birdwatchers, the design of Turtle Creek House was largely developed through its location in terms of its birdlife. The Spencer Theater in New Mexico is 'a sculpted, limestone mass' in tune with the surrounding mountainous terrain. The architect Wendell Burnette, having trained at Taliesin West for three years, works more consciously in a Wrightian tradition than Predock. His, however, is an innovative interpretation of the Wrightian philosophy. In his houses he transforms basic materials to sculptural, sometimes monolithic, effect. Arizona, where he works, possesses an extreme climate that makes environment an unavoidable consideration. This is overlaid by the emphasis that Wendell Burnette, like Predock, places on the awareness of a sense of place.

In 'Design in the Land of "Creative Chaos"' (pages 104–15), Botond Bognar demonstrates how 'new modernism' in Japan can be regarded as occupying a space between modernism and post-modernism, 'having assimilated much of what both have to offer'. This is most marked in changing attitudes to the city: 'The previous aversion to the "disorder" of the Japanese city has been debunked, and its messy vitality, flexibility and resilience discovered'. While the modernism of the 1990s may have shed 1960s modernism's predilection for master plans, urban control and the monumental, it has once again embraced a fixation with constructional innovation and geometrical (or at least non-historicist) forms. The sort of ephemeral and futuristic architecture first proposed by the Japanese Metabolists in the 1960s has also come into its own.

Bognar's choice of schemes exemplifies these trends in Japanese architecture. Tadao Ando's Chikatsu-Asuka Historical Museum, for instance, which was conceived as a man-made hill in a landscape of ancient *kofun* (burial mounds), rejects the sort of monumental modernism espoused in the 1960s and 1970s in favour of a treatment that emphasizes the natural and the phenomenal. Although futuristic, Itsuko Hasegawa's Shonandai Cultural Centre shows a similar predisposition to the natural. The architecture both alludes to nature through its forms, and caters for the inclusion of the natural within it. A hybrid of technological details and nature, it 'reflects the heterogeneous, collage-like texture of the surrounding city'. In his Lyric Hall in Nagaoka, Toyo Ito responds to the Hall's natural setting of rolling hills and distant mountains by defining the building with a long,

15

softly undulating roof, which creates a futuristic form out of one inspired by nature. Fumihiko Maki's Tokyo Gymnasium is another large-scale building which, through its collage-like effect, addresses Tokyo's disparate state. Shin Takamatsu's Kunibiki Messe is comparably monumental in scale. Takamatsu, however, uses light-filled spaces and geometry to breaks up its mass. At night, the emission and reflection of light on the surface contribute to the Matsue skyline.

Despite the disparate voices and varying accounts, the modernism of the 1990s emerges with some constant characteristics. Throughout the world, there is little doubt of its appeal and application in a consumer market. It is, however, a movement that has absorbed the experiences of both its modernist and its post-modernist predecessors. It has cast off the arrogant and overwhelming ardour for the new which was such a feature of the first decades of the Modern Movement – the earliest proponents of the International Style of the 1920s and 30s, in their enthusiasm for the rational and for progress, forsook anything old or traditional. (This attitude was epitomized by the young Le Corbusier who advocated the rebuilding of historic Paris in his Plan Voisin of 1925.) Modernism in the 1990s has been able to harness an admiration for modern forms and technologies with a respect for the existing environment. It has taken on board the criticisms of the post-modern architectural movement of the 1970s and 80s which, as a reaction to the often poorly executed buildings of the postwar years, was largely united by its opposition to a modern language of architecture. Although post-modernism was highly eclectic, ranging from pluralism to classical revivalism, and at its worst constituted the clip-on facades of the commercial buildings of the late 1980s, it also created an atmosphere in which a sensitivity to the environment and the existing urban fabric became a precondition of design.

For Jayne Merkel this is apparent in the taciturn personality of contemporary New York modernism. It responds sensitively and unobtrusively in a historical context. In the western US, this manifests itself in an acute sense of place and sensitivity to the landscape with its ancient sites. In Japan, it can be perceived in the changing attitude to the city, which architects no longer attempt to tame or control, but now admire for its heterogeneity. More than anything, however, it is the call for innovation, the demand for the application of new technology and processes, the urge to reorganize and modernize, that makes 'modern' such an apt word for the present. Architecture comes to the fore at such a moment because the only way to truly express such a *zeitgeist* is to transform interior and exterior built environments to meet the aesthetic desires and current needs of their users.

1 An upper case 'm', tends to be used by writers who regard modernism as an aesthetic style, whereas those who have a broader definition of the modern tend to favour a lower case. For this reason I have used the latter.

2 Ilse Crawford, *Space*, *The Guardian*, 19 September 1997.

3 Michael White, '"Sofa Summit" leaves Antoine sitting pretty', *The Guardian*, 8 November 1997, p14.

4 Fiona Murphy, 'Running on Empty', *The Guardian Weekend*, 30 May 1998, p60.

5 Although both *Elle Decoration* and *Wallpaper* are based in London they are distributed internationally. *Wallpaper* is now owned by the American company Time Inc.

6 'High Cool', *Wallpaper*, January/February 1997, p80.

7 Jennifer Opie, 'The Twentieth Century: Art and Industry', in Reino Liefkes (ed), *Glass*, V&A Publications (London), 1997, p137.

8 Taken from a press release received from the MoMA Design Store by the author, spring 1998.

9 Quoted from 'Walking backwards into the future', *New Socialist*, May 1985 (p21), in Alan Tomlinson, *Consumption, Identity and Style: Marketing, Meaning, and the Packaging of Pleasure*, Routledge (London), 1990, p1.

10 See Ann Douglas, *Terrible Honesty: Mongrel Manhattan in the 1920s*, Picador (London), 1995, p27.

Right Branson Coates, interior of the
'lifestyle' dome, 'powerhouse:: uk',
London, April 1998.

This Government is committed to Britain leading the way into the next millennium
as a creative and forward-thinking nation with whom it is good to do business.
British creativity is at the cutting edge.

We are a world leader in pushing forward the boundaries of art,
design, technology and scientific research.

From fashion to automotive design, from animation to computer games, from
genetic engineering to communications technology, Britain's creative industries are
making a unique contribution.

Our future prosperity as a nation will increasingly depend upon
the success of intangible activities like high technology, design,
financial services and all the creative industries.

John Battle MP   Modern British creativity

Minister of State for Science,

Energy and Industry

When the concept for *Wallpaper** magazine was born in the spring of 1994, one of the first things my creative director asked me was who the magazine was specifically targeted at. 'Tell me who they are,' he coaxed. 'It will be a magazine for urban modernists and global navigators,' I replied. 'An indulgent magazine for men and women, covering interiors, architecture, entertaining and travel, which will be consumed with all things contemporary.'

A little over two years later *Wallpaper** hit newsstands around the world with a cover depicting a sleek-looking Gucci-clad couple lounging in the middle of a simple, white, sun-drenched Manhattan apartment with the singular cover line: urban modernists. It was a tag that immediately became something of a mission statement for the title. Within two words it encapsulated our entire point of view: to focus on all that is modern in metropolitan life.

From architecture to interiors to industrial design we have developed our own in-house definition of what is modern within the context of *Wallpaper**. While there is a degree of elasticity to the term, it covers everything from a spa in Switzerland designed by Peter Zumthor, to a vase crafted by a student at Beckman's art college in Stockholm, to the architecture of 1950s Beirut.

With an agenda which is as much about breaking news as it as about chronicling the work of architects such as Albert Frey, *Wallpaper** is constantly trekking round the globe to document forgotten pockets of modernism that we fear are likely to be demolished by disinterested governments or be renovated beyond recognition by greedy developers.

At the close of this century, modernism, from the perspective of *Wallpaper**'s editors, is all about optimism.

Tyler Brûlé   Creating a magazine for urban modernists

Editor of *Wallpaper**

Top left Launch issue of *Wallpaper**, September/October 1996.

I find it extraordinary that, after seventy years, we are still fighting for the modernist cause. Modernism is still the defining aesthetic of the twentieth century, a response to new technology, new materials and new processes. Yet a common response, especially in Britain, to the challenge of modernism has been a retreat into the cosy fantasies of the past, into the ill-proportioned mock-Georgian estates with their coach lamps and scaled-down ruched blinds. I would agree with William Morris that for traditions to be kept alive, they must not simply be copied, but also be adapted and reworked in a new spirit. The dishonesty of concealing the true functional purpose of things, and the timidity of blindly copying the past, have always made me uneasy. Modernism opens up a new world of possibilities. For me, the importance of modernism is its insistence on space, light and function, and the integration of these into architecture. People became scared at Le Corbusier's idea of the 'machine for living', even though he readily acknowledged that for a space to fulfil its functions – whether as a shop, a house or a garage – it must respond to human needs. This is where, for me, the intellectual process to some extent becomes redundant: homes, offices, libraries, museums, airports, theatres, art galleries and restaurants all depend for their success on how successfully they accommodate the people who use them. We don't (usually) want alien environments; we crave comfort, whether in the physical form of a table, chair or sofa, or in the emotional resonance of a much-loved family heirloom, familiar image or pleasant aroma.

I suppose other people's antipathy to modernism is rather similar to my own antipathy to minimalism. It seems to me that the essential dishonesty of this approach is that it encourages people to believe that the spare emptiness actually reflects how the room functions, when the reality of the situation is that the accessories of everyday life are simply stowed behind almost invisible cupboard doors. Minimalists must eat, dress, cook, work and play like the rest of us, and need things with which to carry out these activities. Architecture and design – when they relate to our homes in particular – must accommodate human, everyday needs. Modernism, I believe, reconciles simplicity with the emotional, spiritual and physical aspects of comfort.

Terence Conran   Modernism

Left The Conran Shop, Michelin Building, London, 1998.

Below Spread from *Elle Decoration*.

Good design and quality are my passions. I believe that people can be stimulated and made happier by their environment, and by using better things. The home can be a pleasure zone.

In British *Elle Decoration*, the magazine I launched in 1991, I have aimed to debunk design and bring high standards, modernity and fresh ideas to a wider audience. It is a magazine that has an influence far in excess of its sales, and is used as a reference by designers and retailers around the world.

Elle Deco's readers trust the magazine to show them what works, and use it as their armchair guide to what to buy. They enjoy their homes and life's little luxuries. They are urban, and work; they own their own place, often as part of a couple. They are part of a big family. These are the sort of people who make choices, and make things happen. Their home is their haven — an intimate world where they can renew themselves, dream, and lead their private lives. They want it to look good, feel right, and work. They are modern, they like to know what's hip but they like their creature comforts too. They are interested in other cultures. They are always on the lookout for things to give spirit to their homes. They want to make informed choices but don't have bags of time to shop around. They've got a life. *Elle Deco* is a magazine about living rather than lifestyle, about easy modern homes rather than cool stylized spaces, about the beautiful everyday.

I believe strongly that our homes should be designed to appeal to us sensually, as well as visually, something that is increasingly necessary to balance the stresses of modern living. I explored some of these ideas in my recent book *Sensual Home*, a modern manual for making the home feel right.

Ilse Crawford   The modern pleasure zone

Founding Editor of British

Elle Decoration

Our aim at IKEA is contribute to a better everyday life for the majority of people.
We do this by offering a wide range of home furnishing items of good design and function, at prices so low that the majority of people can afford to buy them.
People can shop at IKEA for all of their household furnishings – everything from a three-piece suite to a toothbrush holder, and even including the kitchen sink.
It is the ideal way to furnish your home in a modern but affordable way.
As our founder, Invgar Kamprad, puts it: 'Good design isn't really good until it is affordable.'

IKEA   Good modern affordable design

Above IKEA, living room featuring
Stromstad Sofa, 1999.

At its genesis, the Modern Movement was a celebration of social, political and technological progress. It was not whimsical, sceptical, contradictory or timid. It was infused with the spirit of innovation, rose vigorously with coherence and as ever, was greatly opposed. Intellectually and visually demanding, it was uncomfortably unlike architecture which copies the past.

Revolutionaries, political or aesthetic, come under attack for being different; to survive, they deny the history of the immediate past by underlining its contradictions. They build a new ideology out of which myths are created, leaving the ideology open to critical attack.

The postwar, faceless and functional International Style is rooted in the over-simplification of the complex beginning of the Modern Movement. This tendency can be traced to HR Hitchcock and Philip Johnson's 1932 exhibition 'The International Style', held at the Museum of Modern Art, New York, which excluded all architects who were not engaged with finite, reductive white or glass cubes. The nineteenth-century steel pioneers, alongside constructivism, expressionism, futurism, naturalism and plasticism, were all suppressed.

Today many architects are searching beyond the reductivist school. We would wish to be numbered amongst them.

We see our work as the continuation of the Modern Movement, trying to expand its approach to meet constantly changing needs. We are searching for a more open and dynamic, yet harmonious, order which offers the user freedom from the constraints of finite form. It is a geometry which may be modified by new experiences, allowing for planned and unplanned evolution, but in which the totality has complete integrity at any one time.

Richard Rogers   Modernism beyond the reductive

Above Richard Rogers, model of the Millennium Experience, 1998.

Does this new surge of modernism, the new life given to modernist
forms and principles that we see on display throughout this volume,
also mark the end of politics in architectural modernism?
Is it the end of a certain twentieth-century tradition
whereby architecture has been concerned with social change,
with economic progress, with social and, even,
revolutionary activity? Yes and no,
for what we are witnessing here is at once the end of politics in one form, and the resurrection of a politics of another form. This is death and birth as one those great dialectics of modernization, that between production and reproduction, and it seems that the latter is gaining the upper hand.

That modernism has always been infused with political concerns, inspirations and associations is undeniable. From the first battle cry of Filippo Marinetti, Antonio Sant' Elia and the Italian Futurists, singing the song of great crowds, sounds, riots, electric light, power stations and aircraft in the twentieth-century metropolis, modernist architecture has had revolution at its heart. Of course this has not always been revolution of the order of the Bolsheviks and October 1917, and has more often than not sought collusion with the state rather than its overthrowal, but nonetheless modernism has always wanted to change things, and to do so in no small manner. The history of architecture between the two world wars, then, is in effect the history of modernism and social change. On the one hand there were such social democratic, proto-welfarist experiments as those of Ernst May and the housing department of Frankfurt (1925–30), building the housing estates of Römerstadt, Praunheim and Westhausen to accommodate upper-working-class residents. Similar experiments were under-taken at the same time by Bruno Taut, Martin Wagner and Hugo Häring in Berlin, Karl Ehn and Schmidt and Aichinger in Vienna, and Michael Brinkman and JJP Oud in Rotterdam. Berthold Lubetkin and Tecton provided a British equivalent slightly later with the Finsbury Health Centre in London (1935–8). While down another political avenue, the various manifestations of the Bauhaus school in Germany, together with the state-funded RFG research body, sought in the 1920s not just to reform the educa-tion of architects but to alter the social relations of production to include the collaborative endeavours of design, engineering, building construction, craft and aesthetics. Still grander political ambitions were implicated within Le Corbusier's Ville Contemporaine (1922), Ville Radieuse (1935) and Algiers city projects (1930s), for even though Corbusier would happily work with any political grouping to

Resurrection Politics   *Iain Borden*

Modernism and

Architecture in the

Twentieth Century

and Beyond

achieve his architectural ambitions – whether socialist, syndicalist or even the Vichy Government – the political clout necessary to achieve such plans was necessarily large.

Meanwhile, Italy and the US in the 1930s both undertook state-led programmes to regenerate their depression economies and political regimes, involving the construction of new towns, dams, roads and other elements of urban infrastructure. Most significantly of all, the continuing revolution of the young USSR in the 1920s produced true avant-garde activity across all the arts and sciences. The aim was to change not only the modes of production, and the forms that were produced, but also the basic conception of what might constitute architecture and other disciplinary boundaries. Workers' clubs, communications centres, collective apartment blocks and linear towns grew in parallel to new ways of painting, filming, acting, composing and simply living. This was complete political revolution in the making, addressing every aspect of life at its most fundamental grounding.

If this was the victory modernism won for itself in the interwar period, it was a victory that had its most important effects in the postwar years. Here, in the magnificent era of the state, modernism became the universal language for schools, housing, government buildings, theatres, airports, indeed for all metropolitan buildings, in all cities, East and West, across the socialist and capitalist worlds. Some of the better known manifestations of the new bonds between architecture, modernism, the state and the corporate institutions, which by now infiltrated just about every aspect of the urban realm, included: Corbusier at Chandigarh for the Indian state of Punjab (1951–68), Walter Gropius for Harvard University (1950), Ludwig Mies van der Rohe for Seagram in New York (1954–8), Leslie Martin and the Royal Festival Hall for London County Council (1951), the second competition for the Palace of the Soviets in USSR (1957–9), Auguste Perret's reconstruction of Le Havre in France (1945–54), Oscar Niemeyer at Brasilia for the Brazilian government (1957–79), Arne Jacobsen and the National Bank in Copenhagen (1965–71), Kenzo Tange's Plan for Tokyo (1959–60), Gino Valle in Pordenone for Zanussi (1961). Modernism and state politics had become inherently linked, both forming an integral part of the great postwar project for planned economies, planned cities, planned modernization, planned progress, planned health and education, and planned lives.

And yet modernism has always been a critical enterprise, both in itself and through its relation to politics. It is, then, unsurprising that it was precisely in these decades of the omnipotent modernist state that the first signs of a critique of this relation should begin to emerge. While by no means wholly dismissive of the state *per se*, architects such as Alison and Peter Smithson in Britain,

Previous page Branson Coates, Bargo, Glasgow, 1996. Located in a converted warehouse, Bargo plays on the image of the industrial to create a spectacular space of baroque modernity. **Above** Vladimir Tatlin, Monument to the Third International, 1919. Conceived in a period of political optimism and excitement, this tower was revolutionary in its design and its planned use. To be constructed of spiralling steel and glass, 300 metres (900 feet) high, it was intended to contain the worldwide headquarters of the Bolsheviks.

Shadrach Woods in the US, Giancarlo di Carlo in Italy, and Aldo van Eyck and Herman Hertzberger in the Netherlands began to explore a more intimate kind of politics, variously stressing such things as urban place, street life, social associations and collective patterns. Projects such as the Golden Lane Competition Entry (Smithsons, 1952), Frankfurt-Römerberg Competition Entry (Woods, 1963), Student Dormitories in Urbino (Carlo, 1962), Orphanage in Amsterdam (Van Eyck, 1957–60) and school in Delft (Hertzberger, 1966–70) demonstrated a concern with structuralist anthropology, society and historical context and thereby marked a shift from the grand projects of the state to the more integrative politics of local democracy, dispersed power and everyday life. In a somewhat different vein, but still following an implicit critique of the dominance of the state, modernist architects explored such areas as: pop culture and new technology (Archigram, 1961 onwards), a formal investigation of the aesthetic possibilities of modernism (the 'New York Five' of Peter Eisenman, Michael Graves, Charles Gwathmey, John Hejduk and Richard Meier, c1969–72), semiological meanings (Robert Venturi and Denise Scott Brown) and design participation and ecology (Ralph Erskine and Lucien Kroll).

   All of this, of course, has been part of that by now well-known paradigmatic shift from modernism to postmodernism (the latter not necessarily excluding the former) that has accompanied and abetted the corresponding shift from a planned state with a Fordist economy to the much more fractured post-Fordist state and economy. The latter has been characterized by such things as flexible production lines and marketing strategies; globally-dispersed patterns of production tasks and investment; the simultaneous development of regionalized, internationalized and hybridized cultures; an apparent diversification of aesthetics and culture, which has included a 'popularization' of signs and symbols; the increasing commodification of everyday life, including the privatization of public space and the development of hyper-real and simulacra built environments; and a burgeoning bourgeois culture of fear (of crime, of difference, of others). Above all, this has involved a move from an emphasis on an explicitly planned production to an equal emphasis on an apparently free (yet nonetheless highly orchestrated) consumption. We are no longer a society solely of car-makers, medical scientists and agricultural workers but also of movers, carers and restaurant diners, of people who consume as much as they produce, who create attitudes, services and ideas rather than objects, things or facts. And our predominant political agency is correspondingly no longer that of the single controlling state or ruling political party but of the joint venture between self, society, company, institution and government, of a kind of multi-body collective enterprise where unemployment offices are run by Reed

International staff dressed in T-shirts and trainers, and where Coca-Cola sponsors everything from schools to football. We are, in short, at the end of the homogenous state of production, and at the beginning of the fragmented state of consumption.

So what are the politics of this, and how is architectural modernism to respond? Clearly, the old model of the politics of the welfare state, of organized provision, is no longer appropriate. Instead, some modernists have sought radically to revise and extend the old model, seeking to transpose the role of state authority into that democratic partnership of private and public sectors now being conducted by governments in the US and across Europe. Foremost among them is Richard Rogers, whose 1997 book *Cities for a Small Planet* proposes a newly recharged intersection of architecture, ecology and the social life of late twentieth-century cities. If carried out, these ideas would amount to nothing less than a complete overhaul of architectural aesthetics and the spatial planning of cities, redefining 'urbanism' in architecture to incorporate ideas about social justice, environmental responsibility, participatory democracy, globalism and new technologies.

Of course these are not in themselves new ideas, particularly when seen in the context of the history of modernism and politics, but it is extremely rare to find such things being voiced by an architect in the 1990s, and rarer still to see them linked coherently to specific architectural projects. Rogers undertakes sustained attacks not only on the familiar architectural bugbears of 'single-minded spaces', cloyingly nostalgic aesthetics and conservative planning agencies, but also the increasing inequality of wealth distribution, air pollution, global warming, greed, poverty, unemployment, short-term profitism, social alienation and the overarching dominance of the automobile.

In their stead Rogers proposes dense, compact cities with 'open-minded' mixed-use neighbourhoods, composed around public transport nodes. These cities would incorporate participatory planning, environmental education, pollution taxes, 'creative citizenship' for all (especially the young unemployed), parks, squares, renewed existing buildings and wastelands, a revived architectural profession, contrasting architectural aesthetics, and lightweight buildings exploiting natural air and temperature resources. For London, for example, this would mean new Architecture Centres, greater use of the River Thames, a network of cycleways, river buses, efficient and even free public transport, symbolic public buildings, a new elected authority, the re-use of shop and office buildings for housing, and a focus on the inner core of deprivation. All this would be set within an overall urban masterplan to regulate growth.

Above Richard Rogers, Shanghai Pu Dong Model, 1992. The Shanghai model exemplifies Rogers' penchant for a classical, urbane street pattern with plenty of green public space. It centres on a circular plaza or circus dotted with trees from which the main thoroughfares radiate.

Rogers is here serious yet concerned, global yet local, detached yet impassioned, precise yet, occasionally, poetic. His is a magisterial manifesto in the grand modernist tradition of Corbusier's *Urbanisme* of 1925 and Frank Lloyd Wright's *Living City* of 1958, but in its comprehensive social and political motivations it has more in common with urban geographer David Harvey's *Justice, Nature and the Geography of Difference* (1996). At a time when the politics of architecture is increasingly being distracted into arenas of post-structuralist meaning, professional squabbles and single-issue lobbyism – all of which ultimately only serve to send architecture back into itself – this kind of architectural expression is at once necessary and timely.

Yet Rogers' ideas also lend a certain sense of unease, for while they feel largely correct in what they say, the fact of what they leave out, or what they only discursively imply, is the cause of some concern. At the core of this unease is the model of urban living implicit in Rogers' proposals. These are cities of 'civilization' in the oldest sense of the word, meaning 'the art of living in cities'; they are sites of music, theatre, galleries, opera and grand public squares. And while there is the occasional nod to everyday life as being more than just high culture, a certain model of polite society always permeates through. Above all, Rogers' is a city of gentle wanderings, spoken conversations and square-side cafés. It is the city of mocha, big Sunday papers, designer lamps, fresh pasta and tactile fabrics. It is not, however, the city of all the disparate activities that people do in cities. It is not the city of sex, shouting, loud music, running, pure contemplation, demonstrations, subterranean subterfuges. It is not the city of intensity, of bloody-minded determination, of getting out of hand; nor is it the city of cab ranks, boot sales, railway clubs or tatty markets; nor is it the city of monkish seclusion, crystal-clear intellectualism or lonely artistic endeavour.

In physical terms, Rogers' conception of the public city too often seems to mean the urban square. Trafalgar Square, Thames-side walks, tree-lined avenues, Exhibition Road and other London sites are all seen as places for the promenade and the chance encounters of *la passeggiata*. Squares are very pleasant places, but they are far from being a universal panacea to the problems of public space. In Rogers' schema, however, even the proposed Hungerford Bridge is reconceptualized as a 'piazza' from which to view London, thus erasing the qualities of direction, exhilaration, transgression, transience, momentariness and in-betweenness that bridges so uniquely offer.

This may be Rogers' idea of the city – in a newspaper interview he once described his own living room as a piazza – but it is not everyone else's. People of different backgrounds, races,

Right Richard Rogers, Greenwich Peninsula Master Plan, London, 1996. Rogers' Millennium Dome dominates this bird's-eye view of Greenwich with its familiar birthday-cake-like profile. The location of Greenwich, and the dome, in the crook of the River Thames' swerve, is also important for a larger vision of the city. Rogers has long heralded a wider use of the capital's river, both as a focus point and as a means of providing better communications and transport.

ages, classes, sexuality, gender and general interests all have different ideas of public space, and they subsequently use and make their own places to foster their own identities as individuals and citizens. Beyond the square, piazza and avenue, cities need hidden spaces and brutally exposed spaces, rough spaces and smooth spaces, loud spaces and silent spaces, exciting spaces and calm spaces. We as living individuals need spaces in which we encounter otherness and sameness, where we are at once confirmed and challenged. Otherwise we too are erased from view, removed from the square, censured from ourselves, denied the right to the city.

This, then, is where the politics of modernism need to be recharged, along with modernism itself. In effect, the project is to modernize the modernist politics. It is no longer in the politics of homogenous consensus, of the universal man, of high and low culture, of the Sunday square, of right and wrong, that we will find social salvation, but in the politics of difference, of celebrating and emphasizing what Henri Lefebvre has called 'differential space'. In contrast to the homogenizing powers of the abstract space of capitalism, differential space (which is yet to come) will be a more mixed, interpenetrative space, where differences are respected rather than buried under sameness.' According to Lefebvre, differential space will 'put an end to those localizations which shatter the integrity of the individual body, the social body, the corpus of human needs, and the corpus of knowledge.' By contrast, he maintains, 'it will distinguish what abstract space tends to identify – for example, social reproduction and genitality, gratification and biological fertility, social relationships and family relationships.'[12]

Proposals such as Rogers' may well go some way toward such a differential space, but in order to do so there must also be a concomitant development of the modernity of life, of rethinking the human subject, and of our relation to modernism in everyday life.

One indication of how this might happen occurs – in a somewhat ambivalent manner – on the pages of *Wallpaper** magazine. Promoting 'the stuff that surrounds you', this lifestyle journal seems at first sight to treat everything – clothes, food, designer items, places, furniture and so on – as an object. But certain elements set it apart from similar publications. Firstly, modernist architecture and design (some of it deeply unfashionable) is integral to everything it displays: furniture by Florence Knoll; typography by Saul Bass; and, above all, architecture by Paul Rudolph, Albert Frey, RMJM, Oscar Niemeyer, Alvar Aalto, Allies & Morrison, Richard Seifert and so forth, are its preferred tastes. Secondly, modernist design is embedded into the very lives of the magazine's (semi-fictionalized) consumers. This is not modernist architecture and design as we see it in books, in the art gallery or in

Right Bernard Tschumi, Parc de La Villette, Paris, 1984. This scheme saw the realization of some of Tschumi's theoretical ideas. Deconstructivist red pavilions, or *folies*, are dotted around a science park. **Opposite above** Branson Coates, Bargo, Glasgow, 1996. **Opposite below** Koning Eizenberg Architecture, OP12 5th Street Housing, Los Angeles, 1987. Mixing private and public housing, this estate demonstrates that modernism with a social conscience is still a viable force in contemporary architecture.

the university lecture room, but brought within the realm of the contemporary metropolis. Thirdly, and most importantly, there is politics at work here. Now this is also where *Wallpaper** can get a little tricky, for it generally promotes a kind of affluent elitism that revels in the relative affluence and youth of its chic, LA–New York–London–Berlin–Milan–Tokyo–axis metropolitan readership. But its politics are there nonetheless, not so much in the objects themselves but in the pictorial and textual narratives that it weaves in and around these objects. It is a politics of sexuality. The models are men and women of unstated sexuality, probably gay but not explicitly so. The storylines suggest sex without showing it, with rumpled bed clothes, multiple bodies of indeterminate relationships and suggestive strap lines such as 'Hard and Fast', 'Behind the Screens' or 'Some Like It Off'.[3] Above all, in encouraging people to 'sort out your space', they invoke the individual's independence, suggest that they can be who they want to be – with modernist design, or course, being an intrinsic part of the new social construction.[4]

Of course, we would not want all the world to be a *Wallpaper** world. But (albeit when viewed with a healthy dose of irony) the magazine does show a fragment, the merest glimpse of how modernism might be part of an individual's personal world, how it might play a part in each person's celebration of difference, and of life itself. In a way, this can be seen as a return to some of the earliest moments of modernism (Adolf Loos, Otto Wagner) and to its most far-reaching social interventions (the German *existenzminimum*, Aalto, Le Corbusier, Ludwig Hilberseimer), where modernism was not just about the modernization of the world but also about the concept of 'modernity', the experience of the modern. Similar glimpses may also be seen in the symbolically loaded theatricality, discord and narrative of Branson Coates' bars and shops; in the social consciousness of firms such as Koning Eizenberg Architecture in Los Angeles, who mix expensive residences with non-profit work for affordable housing or single-room occupancy accommodation; and in the theorizations of Bernard Tschumi for a politics of space, pleasure and architecture.

Above all, the implication of the above-mentioned designers and projects is that ultimately what matters is not the building itself but our experience of it. Thus, human beings might be characterized less as the users and inhabitants of architecture and more as its subjects, who 'reproduce' it through consuming it. This is what produces a truly lived-in architecture, and hence also a true politics of modernity. Marshall Berman has defined modernism as 'any attempt by modern men and women to become subjects as well as objects of modernization, to get a grip on the modern world and make themselves at home in it'.[5] This is the real challenge for a politics of modernism in architecture.

1 Henri Lefebvre, *The Production of Space*, Blackwell (Oxford), 1991, pp48–50, 52, 60 and 409.
2 Lefebvre, *The Production of Space*, p52.
3 *Wallpaper**, May/June 1998.
4 *Wallpaper**, March/April 1998.
5 Marshall Berman, *All That is Solid Melts into Air: the Experience of Modernity*, Penguin (Harmondsworth, Middlesex), 1988, p5.

We are modern now. This is not just a question of style, but a cultural shift.
There have been deep-rooted changes in the way we live
which mean that modern is the way we want to be.
This is a new modernity, however, one that is tailored to the needs
of the decade some have dubbed the 'Neurotic Nineties'.
The most obvious change, in Britain at least, is the political one.
For the first time in nearly twenty years there is a Labour government in power,
and at a time of relative prosperity. It is a party with a young(ish) leadership, but more importantly a political party that tactically wants to be seen to associate itself with forward-looking creativity in music, architecture, art and so on, rather than the forces of the establishment. (Whether or not that talent actually wants to be associated with the new government is a separate issue.) The British government has looked to modern thinkers such as architect Richard Rogers, to advise on housing, and Nigel Coates, to design the 'powerhouse::uk' exhibition for the April 1998 Asian summit. This has all helped to change the status quo from one where modernity is seen as a threat, to one where it seems exciting.

Much of this is down to the power and influence of members of the 'baby boom' generation in the US and Britain, who are now in their late thirties and early forties. They have become the new establishment. Paradoxically, many of these people benefited from the opening-up of opportunities that occurred under Thatcher's Britain, and now have the money and power to make a difference. They are men and women who grew up with popular culture, with the Clash and Iggy Pop, with Vivienne Westwood, with street fashion and magazines like *The Face*. They are older now, with more responsibilities perhaps, but inside they are the same people they were when they were twenty. These are the people for whom the marketing term 'middle youth' was invented. They don't want to grow old. They dress fashionably, still do drugs and go out on the razzle (and then take vitamins by the bucket load, or maybe go to the gym) and like to try to keep up to speed on contemporary culture. They want a piece of the present, a slice of the future in order to advertise their connection to things cool and modern, to sidestep middle-age and stay forever young. Modernity represents optimism and a sense of forward-thinking. The baby boomers do not want to surround themselves with the traditional, with things that might remind them of that dreaded word, 'old'.

But what is modern now? After all, the concept was introduced nearly a century ago, and has been defined primarily by men.' Earlier this century it meant a vision of a technological future,

All Modern   *Ilse Crawford*

and Emotional

New Designs for

British Living

but now that we actually live in a technological age, definitions have shifted. Today we need our homes to provide a balance to the insecurities and the hard edges of the mechanical world around us, while incorporating all the advantages and visual excitement of modernity. And this 'newly modern' generation of people in their thirties and forties provides the bridge between the old world and the new, between what was and what will be. At times, that that can be a pretty uncomfortable position.

The last decade or so has been a time of massive social change; our lives and our expectations have been transformed. In the late 1990s, everything that was previously certain seems to be in flux. An important factor has been the so-called 'feminization' of society. In the US and Britain in particular, more women work than ever before, and the number is on the increase. They are better paid and better educated than before, and are delaying having children (if indeed they have them at all). The money and preferences of these so-called 'genderquakers' are changing the status quo.

One side effect is the rising divorce rate; in Britain close to one in two marriages end in divorce. Seventy per cent of these divorces are initiated by women, who are now sufficiently financially independent to go it alone. Among other things, this means the number of single-occupancy households is on the increase. It follows that the family unit is not what it was; serial monogamy seems to be replacing it as the modern domestic arrangement. In this climate, the romantic vision of the traditional family home – complete with Aga stove, Laura Ashley and home-baked cookies – has less allure. Whether or not we have children, our homes are more likely to reflect our immediate personal taste and needs, rather than any idea of building a future. The family, it seems, has now become a combination of individuals.

The way in which we work has also changed. The very nature of employment has been revolutionized: the idea of the long-term corporate ladder has gone and people are taking command of their own futures. There is a trend towards working from home, at least some of the time, and so homes must be able to function on this level too. And not only do both men and women work, but we work (it seems) all the time. In Britain we now work longer hours than in any other European country (this is particularly so for professionals), hence the biggest pressure on our lives these days is time – or, rather, the lack of it. The workplace and the service industries have yet to adapt significantly to these radical social changes, so time is our most valuable commodity. It is seen as the enemy, something to work against. Today there is no time for high-maintenance homes. We want our domestic spaces to be low or even no maintenance, so that we can spend our limited leisure time with friends

Previous page The home of art director, Doug Lloyd, New York, featured in *Elle Decoration*, February 1998. With its bare white walls and hard wood floors, the loft apartment creates a neutral backdrop for its sensuous contents: a collection of modern furniture, Scandinavian ceramics and photography. **Above** Cover for *Elle Decoration*, June 1998. Neil Logan and Solveig Fernlund's loft conversion in SoHo, New York, for an artist and film-maker, displays their advocation of a contemporary brand of Scandinavian modernism, mixing craft and colour with stark spaces.

and families rather than doing the laundry. The use of domestic help has consequently escalated dramatically over the past few years.

What we want from our houses is different, too. We need homes where we can live our modern lives, rather than fight against an Edwardian way of living that is no longer relevant. People today are looking at the very shape of how we live and adapting it accordingly. No wonder there is a drift back to the inner cities, to industrial spaces that we can 'cut to fit'. The way we use our living environment has changed; we now require at least some flexible, multi-purpose space. We have to juggle different tasks – working, cooking, talking to friends, keeping an eye on the children – and need a space that will allow us to do this. Separate dining rooms, sitting rooms and drawing rooms are pointless if in the few hours that you are at home you only use the kitchen and the bedroom. The situation is even worse if couples spend the only time they have together at opposite ends of the house.

Emotionally, too, we demand more of our homes. Today's women have different values to the traditional male ones which have dominated our conception of the modern. The picture is changing: a recent Demos report identifies a move towards greater ease, individualism, empathy, spiritualism, hedonism and fulfilment.[2] Women, it would seem, want their homes to soothe and excite, to connect to their sense of self and their emotions, to constitute a stage in their life story rather than act as a showpiece of status or a symbol of domesticity. Women may well like modernity, but they often have a different interpretation of it than do their male colleagues. More often than not they would agree with designer Eileen Gray's comment on the work of her contemporaries Jean Prouvé, Le Corbusier et al: 'Avant-garde architecture has no soul'. To quote travel writer Dea Birkett, whose words could equally well be applied to attitudes to the home: 'Men want to conquer the territory they travel through and plant a flag on it. But women want to be conquered by the territory, to be enchanted and intrigued by it.'

The shift towards more 'female' values is increasingly true for men as well as for women. Men in many corporations are fighting for more time with their families, while women are increasingly the major wage-earners. Our homes are one of the few areas in our lives that we do (usually) have control over, and as such provide a haven where we can balance the stresses of the outside world, at the same time as basking in the reflected glory of our personal style.

There will increasingly be many different sorts of modernity to accommodate many different ways of life. It is thus that we find ourselves entering an age of 'soft modernity'. This is a more

Right Iain Halliday, conversion of 1960s suburban house, Sydney, featured in *Elle Decoration*, June 1997. This house combines a desire for the modern with a response to family needs. The double-storey kitchen-cum-living space is the heart of the home, as well as a setting for a contemporary art and furniture collection.

inclusive and hedonistic spin on the modern; one that allows for apparent contradictions — we fill industrial kitchens with peasant bowls, place cashmere shawls on an Eames lounger, and have delicate, pretty sheets on a minimal bed. It is sensual and emotional rather than rational and cutting-edge. As we demand more pleasure from our homes we become more skilled and sensitive in our use of colour, light and texture. It can be a decorated modernity that accommodates the changing world we live in. We are a well-travelled, multi-racial society and enjoy references to other cultures, things brought back from far-off places or simply the buzz of something new and strange from somewhere else. Modern seems perfectly fine with elaborate or kitsch stuff from India, China or North Africa. Handmade objects now have a romantic charm to them; no longer the 'enemy', they have become an endangered species, and we value them for that. They, too, have a place in our modern worlds. This new relationship with nature and the natural enables us to integrate it within urban life.

Sure enough, retailing and the media have lost no time in satisfying this new craving. Modernity has never been more accessible and affordable — and new fads and enthusiasms travel fast. Trends that used to take several years to percolate through are now on the high street in a matter of months. What for years have been the preserve of the well-heeled in-classes is now available to the many (in 1999 Habitat UK will be selling designs by Verner Panton, Robin Day and Castiglione, for instance). Wherever you look there is media coverage, in magazines and on television. Good design and architecture can be seen on a daily basis in bars and restaurants, while an increasing number of retailers and individual designers sell better and better products. High-quality modern design, and the things that go with it, have never been more widely available. Even the fashion industry — masters of the marketing machine — has now jumped on board, with many top-name designers now having their own home collections.

The modern of the late 1990s, then, is about tying your colours to the future, as well as dealing with some of the more pressing practical demands of the present. We are modern because we have to be, as well as because we want to be. It is about living with paradox, about bringing together ideas that had previously been seen to be in opposition. It is modernity with the edges knocked off. Our homes must be easy and modern, while also taking their creature comforts seriously. They must at the same time be practical and adaptable, because the needs of everyday life are tricky enough to negotiate without creating yet more handicaps. And, of course, they must be contemporary. Heaven forbid that we should look old-fashioned.

Opposite The New York home of James Gager and Richard Ferretti, featured in *Elle Decoration*, July/August 1997. The wholly white apartment has the impact of a black and white photograph, with its heightened sense of light and shade.

1 I take Adolf Loos's 1908 article 'Ornament and Crime' as the starting-point for modernity.
2 Helen Wilkinson and Melanie Howard, *Tomorrow's Women*, Demos.

'Light and air', the rallying call of the pioneer modernists, was largely directed at 'serious' building types such as workers' housing and community colleges. There was little emphasis on applying modernist thinking to more 'frivolous' buildings for entertainment – such as theatres or restaurants – until after 1945, when a new generation of modern architects turned their attention to aspects of the modern project not directly concerned with social struggle.

The groundbreaking results of this period can be seen internationally in such landmark schemes as Jørn Utzon's Sydney Opera House (1956), Denys Lasdun's Royal National Theatre in London (1967) and Fumihiko Maki's National Museum of Modern Art in Kyoto (1986).

One of the chief characteristics of the 'new modernism' of the 1990s, especially in the British context, is the reapplication of 'light and air' to cultural buildings associated with consumption, as opposed to those associated with production, shelter and education. Retail and leisure designers, in particular, have embraced the modernist doctrine afresh to revitalize a consumer palette jaded by the over-rich historicist diet of post-modernism in the late 1980s.

This is particularly evident in the recent London restaurant boom. Popular new eateries have sprung up all over the capital, many featuring the trademark signatures of the 'new modernism' in form, space and light – especially the use of artificial light. This essay makes comparisons between three recent London restaurant schemes, each of which reveals a different interpretation of a singular bold modernist vision of 'light and air'.

First, there is Sir Terence Conran's 700-seater Mezzo (1993) on the original site of the Marquee Club in the West End – a spectacular study in Art Deco-tinged moderne interior design, with mirrored walls, pale surfaces, white tablecloths and gleaming chrome helping to reflect light into every corner. Second, there is the 220-seater Bank (1996) at the Aldwych, designed by Julyan Wickham, with its subtle, almost surreal modern design – an utterly contemporary construct epitomized by its Hopperesque murals and continuous green glass chandelier suspended above its diners. A third scheme – the restoration of Italian restaurant Bertorelli's (1996) by architects Harper Mackay – recaptures the intimate sensuality of a 1950s Milanese trattoria in its detailing and evokes that special period of immediate postwar Italian modernism, the era of *reconstruzione*. This is especially apparent in a series of beguiling, colourful, fluorescent-lit display boxes of woven timber inset into the fabric of the main dining area.

Light, Air and the   *Jeremy Myerson*

Modernist Menu

Three London

Restaurants

Between the grand theatrical approach of Mezzo, with its 1920s undertones; the quirky styling of Bank, with its hint of Eliot Noyes' East Coast America and that mid-century fixation with abstract impressionism; and the more casual intimacy of Bertorelli's, reflecting the particular penchant of the postwar Italian modernists to find a way to relax within the genre, we see the range of cultural influences on the 'new modernism' in Britain. We also see the range of resultant interior forms, showing that if modernism is no longer the true universal type, it remains more than just one of a series of historically accessible, deadweight styles. It has the genuine capacity to surprise and delight with each reinvention and reinterpretation. Indeed London's restaurants – not just these three but also Conran's Quaglino's and Bluebird Café, Ron Arad's Belgo Centraal, Damien Hirst's Pharmacy, Rick Mather's Avenue, and Marc Newson's Coast and Mash – collectively reflect a modern spirit with a lot of life in it yet. In each case, the relationship between space and light makes a defining contribution to the visual experience of the diner. This relationship, of course, has always been central to the success of Terence Conran's London restaurants. The designer and retailer who with his Habitat-Mothercare business owned half the British high street in the 1980s, has in the 1990s reinvented himself as a master restaurateur. Every month, it seems, new Conran restaurants open across town.

The project which really signalled Conran's renaissance as a 1990s designer and entrepreneur – after his publicly quoted retail empire had foundered on the rocks of recession – was his theatrical Quaglino's, opened in 1993. On this 1,400 square metre (15,000 square foot) project, Conran worked with interior designers Keith Hobbs and Lizi Coppick, and lighting designers and contractors Marlin, who created an ingenious illuminated skylight which runs the length of the basement eaterie and is seasonally adjusted to emulate the patterns of natural light. Every detail, from the sinuous curves of counters and balustrades to the Q-shaped ashtrays and cigarette girls in 1920s costumes, reflects Conran's love affair with French culinary culture in a brisk Art Deco-flavoured setting.

At Mezzo, Conran set out to capture the glamour of Quaglino's but on a far larger scale. Again he collaborated with the same lighting design team from Marlin. The result is a spectacular scheme which overcomes the potential for gloom of the former Marquee Club with its vast scale. The main lighting is unobtrusively provided by low voltage tungsten halogen downlights, all on individual transformers. A sophisticated dimming system allows staff total flexibility in setting light levels. The interior design emphasis is on reflecting light into every corner – aided by the combination of mirrored walls, pale surfaces, white tablecloths and gleaming chrome. Before Mezzo opened, Conran

explained his vision for the venue: 'I hope Mezzo gives people such a thrill that their jaws drop when they see it for the first time.' A key part of the drama of Mezzo is the kitchen areas, which are open to the view of diners. Here, the lighting is necessarily functional, in contrast to the more decorative lighting approach in the restaurant. Fibre optics also plays a role, downlighting one intimate, enclosed dining area, and enhancing the innovative design of an upstairs bar.

Conran's success with Quaglino's and Mezzo not only encouraged him to open more venues, it also inspired a new generation of restaurateurs to serve up something new for London. Tony Alan and Ron Truss of Marchthistle are behind the 940 square metre (10,100 square foot) Bank restaurant, which has caught the imagination for two main reasons. First is its somewhat unusual location on the outer fringes of theatreland at the Aldwych; some initially thought it was too far off the beaten track but the local legal and management consulting community have given it a warm welcome. The second point of interest is architect Julyan Wickham's confident, colourful modern interior design. Wickham had to find a way to overcome the site's awkward hourglass shape and extreme spatial depth. He does so with a single inspired lighting intervention that is at once full of bravado and sensitivity. A continuous horizontal lighting chandelier leads diners to the rear of the restaurant and unifies the space. Weighing over 20 tons, it is composed of a polar landscape of 2,800 individually shaped and numbered greenish glass fins. Likened to the shimmering underside of a slowly melting glacier, it competes for attention in a space dominated by two vast murals by Wickham's daughter Pola.

Much of the appeal of Bank lies in its juxtaposition of a sophisticated plan with almost cartoon-like colours and forms. A linear kitchen, screened by a glass wall, runs down the middle of the restaurant uniting the two widest points of the hourglass. One end presents a semi-circular bar with full-height glazing to the street; the other becomes the venue's food service station. Vibrant shades of blue, red, yellow and orange on walls and columns combine with Wickham's own custom seating designs to project a modernist interpretation that is lively, diverse and quirky, and in which the main glacier-chandelier, designed by the architect using concealed lamps, holds the key.

Like Wickham Associates at Bank, architects Harper Mackay designed their scheme for Bertorelli's in the spirit of the modern. But while the creative ambition and attention to detail was similar, the aims of the project were very different. Whereas Bank was an entirely new enterprise which needed to make a big splash quickly, Bertorelli's is one of London's most established restaurants and

Previous page Terence Conran, Mezzo, London, 1993. The dramatic circular staircase leading down to the basement restaurant creates the main focus of the space. This demands a sense of the theatrical as customers are unable to avoid making a conspicuous entrance. **Opposite and right** Julyan Wickham Associates, Bank, London, 1996. In both the restaurant and bar areas, the chandelier with its glazed fins predominates. A highly ingenious solution to an oddly shaped site, the chandelier draws the eye, creating a continuous flow of space.

needed to refurbish and renew its appeal in the face of all the brash designer newcomers in the field. With its bentwood chairs and aproned waitresses of a certain age, the old Bertorelli's had in the words of designer Ken Mackay, 'the disciplinary brown tones of a school refectory'.

Harper Mackay's scheme cost £1 million and involved the total refit of a gross area of 620 square metres (6,700 square feet). It entailed moving the old atrium to the back of the building where it could take natural light into the formerly dimly-lit eating areas. This atrium is overlooked by glass partitions leading to function rooms; this and the mirror cladding on the rear walls enable different dining areas to enjoy a visual relationship while maintaining acoustic separation. It is in the main dining areas that Harper Mackay has really made its mark. The wall finish in the first-floor restaurant and ground floor Café Italian is a woven lattice of veneered plywood strips of maple and American black oak, inset with brightly coloured display boxes containing glass and ceramics lit by concealed fluorescent tubes. The contrast between dark veneered wood and glowing boxes has a retro feel reminiscent of Italian trattoria and cappuccino bars of the 1950s and 60s. Curiously, it is the decorative work of this period which so inspired the Memphis collections of Ettore Sottsass in Milan in the early 1980s, one of the main groundsprings of post-modernism in interior and product design.

'We wanted to give the walls depth and make them more intriguing,' explains Ken Mackay, whose team worked closely with the electrical contractors on the project. Elsewhere, the interior scheme is predominantly discreet and the lighting low voltage. The architects' flamboyance has been reserved for the exterior treatment, where recessed and exposed fittings highlight the new fascia. Bertorelli's is a project which uses light, space and detail to combine old and new architecture in a modern way, one which is comfortable but never predictable. The new interiors are very much of the 1990s, but in a gesture to long-time regulars who are sentimental about the restaurant's heritage, the old Bertorelli's sign has been brought inside and mounted at the back of the Café Italian.

While Mezzo shows that mass catering can be highly stylish, and Bank shows that an unusual location is no barrier to success if the design (and to a lesser extent the food) is right, Bertorelli's shows that faded venues can be given vibrant new life without destroying their original spirit. All three restaurants reflect in different ways the old modernist rallying cry of 'light and air'. But they do so through the filter of a modernist experience which has embraced so much cultural and geographical variation over the past seventy years that one cannot talk of the 'new modernism' as a singular style — even if it perhaps reflects a singular attitude to improve and impress.

Above, right and opposite Harper Mackay, Bertorelli's, London, 1996. In this modernization of a well-known Italian restaurant, Harper Mackay was able to preserve some references to its earlier incarnations. The original Bertorelli's sign (above), for instance, has been hung up on a wall in the Café Italian, in the basement of the restaurant. The detailing evokes the modernism of the 1950s — when Italian café culture was in its prime — with its use of maple and American black oak veneer on walls punctuated with back-lit niches (opposite), as well as brightly coloured furniture.

By the 1980s, critics and academics were declaring modernism well and truly dead.[1] The modernist-inspired rebuilding of Britain after the Second World War had never been a great success with the public at large. Lionel Escher in his 1981 book *A Broken Wave* summarized the situation: 'The English reacted against the black-and-white world of modernism exactly as they had reacted against the cream-and-black world of the Regency: they wished to shed the stiff shirt and tails and get back into woollens. And when the inevitable entropy overtook the black-and-white world and it all turned grey, reaction turned to revolt.[2]

Although pioneering attacks had been led against modernism in the 1960s and 1970s, most notably by Robert Venturi and Charles Jencks, it only became an issue for heated popular debate during the 1980s.[3] When in 1981 the American journalist and writer Tom Wolfe wrote in his highly readable tract, *From Bauhaus to our House,* that 'modern architecture is exhausted, finished', he seemed to be voicing a widely held public view.[4] In Britain, the Prince of Wales was looked to as the figurehead of traditional architecture and anti-modernism. This was brought about largely by his famous 1984 condemnation of Ahrends Burton and Koralek's plans for the extension of the National Gallery, while speaking at the Royal Institute of British Architecture's 150th anniversary dinner, as 'a monstrous carbuncle on the face of a much-loved and elegant friend'. This was a gift for the British media in the late 1980s, who played an active part in fanning anti-modernist sentiments. Their involvement reached its height with the controversy over the redevelopment of Paternoster Square in the City of London, a postwar modernist scheme adjacent to St Paul's Cathedral. When in August 1987, Arup Associates' modern design was announced the winner of a select competition to produce a master plan for the redevelopment of the square, London's *Evening Standard* jumped in and championed the public's and Prince Charles's prejudices by providing funds for an alternative Classical Revival scheme by John Simpson.[5]

Death, however, is a necessary prerequisite to any ensuing revival, resuscitation or resurrection. If modernism was deemed to have outrightly failed in the 1980s, this helped to secure its comeback in the 1990s. Any cultural movement that is condemned or rejected by the establishment eventually becomes an irresistible draw to practitioners working outside the mainstream, and to students and young architects.

In Britain, modernism was deemed to have failed in the 1970s and 80s partly because of its association with the welfare state, which was also regarded as bankrupt. As Adrian

Burning up the Years   *Helen Castle*

The Revival of British

Modernism in the 1990s

Forty has written in his essay on the perceived failure of modernism, 'the label of failure has been reserved almost exclusively for works built by the state'.[6] At this time, public indignation was particularly focused on social housing schemes, most stereotypically high-rise flats, which were regarded as eyesores as well as being technically flawed. It was only in the late 1960s, however, that modern housing emerged as a political issue. Prior to that, the drive for new housing cut across political party lines as the construction of homes was regarded as expedient to postwar reconstruction – and the higher density, the better.

The Conservative government, however, in due course came to disassociate themselves from high-rise building. Miles Glendinning and Stefan Muthesius describe in *Tower Block* how this came to pass: 'This change of local-political opinion against the Modern housing drive was not gradual, but burst into the open in the context of the sweeping victories of Conservatives and other nonsocialist groups in the 1967–8 municipal elections. In the first systematic party-political use of issues concerning the architectural form of housing, Conservatives in many municipalities branded large-scale clearance and multi-storey building a "Socialist" policy, and on their accession to power, moved quickly to cut output and increase the number of improvement schemes'.[7]

In the 1980s, the denunciation of modern forms of social housing was consolidated by Margaret Thatcher's Conservative government, which set about selling off council houses as part of a wider objective to dismantle the welfare state and privatize national industries.

What is most remarkable about the modernism of Britain in the 1990s is the way it seems to have shed all of its previous baggage. This has happened to such an extent that some postwar housing developments – albeit the best designed and most centrally located (such as Chamberlin, Powell & Bon's mid-1950s Golden Lane Estate, near London's Barbican) – have been rejuvenated as sought-after pied-à-terres by design professionals.[8] More to the point, the modernist work that is now being designed and built has been able to free itself from its previous associations. Modernism has been successfully commodified by architects and applied to commercial spaces such as the interior of clothes shops and restaurants. Its use is particularly marked in London's restaurants (see Jeremy Myerson's essay, pages 36–41) and at the top end of the retail trade: you only have to walk down Bond Street to see the impact it has had. Once again, there is a strong parallel with politics; where 'old Labour' was associated with an outmoded socialism during the 1980s, the party has now been reborn as a vital force, and one that freely embraces capitalism.

Previous page Michael Hopkins & Partners, interior of Glyndebourne Opera House, Sussex, 1994. After the wilderness years of British modernism, the prestigious commission of a building such as the new opera house at Glyndebourne signified a confidence in new architectural solutions by the British establishment. Finely crafted and acoustically engineered, the inside of the auditorium is often likened to a musical instrument. The sense of being within the body of a string instrument, such as a violin or lute, is enforced by its lining of reclaimed pitched pine panels.

The high-tech movement The 1980s saw nothing short of a transformation in the general perception of modernism in Britain. From being a movement associated with poor planning, new towns and tower blocks that poison the view, it became regarded as a sophisticated urban style. Responsibility for this turnaround in modernism's fortunes lies to a large extent with the high-tech, an approach to architecture developed during the 1970s, most notably by Richard Rogers and Norman Foster. By 1985, Richard Rogers had declared: 'I believe in the rich potential of modern industrialist society. Aesthetically one can do what one likes with technology for it is a tool, not an end in itself, but we ignore it at our peril.'[9]

Rogers' emphasis on an 'industrialist' society is particularly interesting. Rogers, at this time, was working on Lloyds of London (completed 1986), a building that housed one of the City's most important financial houses. Rogers was quite openly aligning himself with a high-tech modernism that embraced modern commerce. For him and for other modernist architects this was quite a shift in ideology. Only ten years earlier, he and his partner, Renzo Piano, when working on the construction of the Centre Pompidou in Paris (1970–7), had made a call for social revolution: 'Ideology cannot be divided from architecture. Change will clearly come from radical changes in social and political structures … the aim of technology is to satisfy the needs of all levels of society. Technology cannot be an end in itself but must aim at solving long-term social and ecological problems.'[10] Norman Foster, Rogers' former partner in the British firm Team 4, also made his international reputation with a headquarters for an insurance company, the Willis Faber & Dumas Building in Ipswich (1975) and in the mid-1980s was completing the Hongkong and Shanghai Bank Headquarters, Hong Kong (1986).

Although the high-tech can be regarded as having its roots in the geodesic domes of Richard Buckminster Fuller and the paper fantasies of Archigram, it also responds to the nineteenth-century engineering tradition of British railway stations with their vast spans of glass and iron. As Michael Sorkin has written: 'Rogers does represent the apogee of some kind of optimism, the happy Brunelian satisfactions of spanning long and visibly.'[11] This was a tradition that was not only highly pragmatic in its use of materials, but also in its aims; it represented an industrial and ultimately entrepreneurial culture.

To some degree the secret of high-tech's success lay in its independence from state-commissioned work and its early application to private monumental projects. By the 1980s, there was already a history of detachment from the public sector. Colin Rowe has described the extent to which James Stirling, the author of the proto high-tech work the Leicester Engineering Building (1959), should be seen against such a background of 'dissent'.[12] For as early as 1951, the picturesque modernism of the 1950s, which became the prescribed style of the Festival of Britain, the *Architectural Review* and the architects of the welfare state, proved itself too 'local, chauvinist and totally restricting' for him.[13] At Leicester, like the succeeding generation of high-tech architects, Stirling chose to use the Modern Movement for his own means. Nothing could be further from the strange marriage of the rational Bauhaus and the populist 'attractive' planning that constituted the postwar picturesque modernism, than Leicester's gritty alliance of 'the canonical forms of the Modern Movement with elements drawn from the industrial vernacular of Stirling's native Liverpool'.[14]

By the 1980s, however, most of the high-tech movement's major achievements were for foreign clients. The British architectural press was constantly bemoaning the fact that our best architects had to work abroad. Even in 1995, Samantha Hardingham in her compilation of contemporary British architectural projects stated that 'many of our architects look abroad for significant commissions'.[15] In the same year, only £3 million of the £16 million turnover of Foster Holdings came from the UK.[16] There also remained the problem of building in more sensitive contexts or urban sites, where the traditionalist and post-modernists generally seemed to gain the upper hand. By the late 1980s and early 1990s, the high-tech architects were starting to produce buildings that were winning international acclaim both for their sensitivity and their imaginative solutions.

In 1991, the same year as Venturi Scott Brown's Sainsbury Wing of the National Gallery opened (to the Prince of Wales' approval), Foster Associates' Sackler Galleries in the Royal Academy were completed. They represented a triumph for modern architecture in one of the most architecturally sensitive and traditionally conservative institutions in London. Foster's scheme acts as a seam between two historic buildings. It centres on a gap of 5 metres (5½ feet) between Samuel Ware's garden facade of 1815 and Sidney Smirke's gallery extension of 1867, in which a circulation space, stairwell and lift are inserted. At its upper level an entrance was also created to the renovated Diploma Galleries (renamed the Sackler Galleries). By cleaning the existing facades, and inserting between them an architecture that exceeded itself in its use of fine materials – glass and steel stairs, a glass-walled lift, stone floors – it was able to conserve the structure and the proportions of the existing building, if anything making it even more of a focus to visitors as they were brought into closer contact with the nineteenth-century brickwork.

Right Foster Associates, Sculpture Gallery, Sackler Galleries, Royal Academy of Arts, London, 1991. Norman Foster's design for the RA solved the problem of creating new structures within a historical context by its emphasis on transparency. This gallery, which acts as an entrance for the new Sackler Galleries, displays some of the Academy's prize exhibits such as the Michelangelo *tondo*. It acts as a viewing gallery in more ways than one, since the glazed wall, floor and ceiling reveal to the visitor the interface of the building's two existing facades.

Another high-tech practice that has proved its ability to juxtapose historic buildings with highly innovative architecture is that of Michael Hopkins & Partners. In 1987, it had already displayed such a sensibility in its Mound Stand at Lord's Cricket Ground, where the practice was responsible for the restoration and completion of the existing facade of 1898 at ground level, as well as the cantilevered steel-framed seating decks above and the tensile structures that form the roofs. It was at Glyndebourne Opera House (1994), however, that Hopkins really succeeded in winning over the establishment. Adjacent to a country house, situated in the heart of the Sussex Downs, it is the venue for an opera festival that is traditionally part of the summer social season: in formal evening dress, people picnic on the lawn in front of the house. Oval in plan, the opera house takes the form of a round house (not unlike nineteenth-century round houses used for turning railway engines). The auditorium has a concrete and steel structure, but is surrounded by a load-bearing brick drum. The pale pink of the handmade Hampshire bricks, combined with the extensive use of reclaimed pitch pine inside the auditorium, displays the sort of truth and passion for materials extolled by the Modern Movement. Its simplicity and strength also lie in its omissions – it dares to dispense with the type of flourishes, stucco work and rich upholstery that typify the interiors of British theatres, so that its implied luxury hinges on its refined specification of materials and design.

The rejuvenation of modernism The Sackler Galleries and Glyndebourne would seem to suggest that by the beginning of the 1990s, high-tech architects were prepared to be the exponents of a more subdued approach within a historical context. But around this time other commissions did start to emerge which required the projection of an essentially forward-looking image. One such highly acclaimed and popular scheme was Nicholas Grimshaw & Partners' Waterloo International Terminal (1993). As the main terminal building of the new train link with Paris, via the Channel Tunnel, it was perceived as the 'Gateway to Europe'. The most prominent feature of Grimshaw's design is its glass roof. It alludes to the optimism of the heroic, nineteenth-century age of train travel – as epitomized by the stations of British engineers, with their vast glass and iron spans – at the same time as endowing the structure with a futuristic covering and signature. A vast scaly sleeve of glass, the roof covers the Eurostar platforms in a flattened three-pin bowstring arch, which is distorted to follow the changing widths of the platforms below. In its passage it uncompromisingly clips the corner of any flats and office blocks that stand in its way.

Above Michael Hopkins & Partners, Glyndebourne Opera House, Sussex, 1994. In the foreground can be seen the bay window of the nineteenth-century neo-Elizabethan country house, which hosts the opera in its gardens. Although the new auditorium takes its own innovative form, its circular shape and the use of pink hand-made bricks acknowledge the presence of the adjacent house. **Right** Nicholas Grimshaw & Partners, Waterloo International Terminal, London, 1993. Viewed from the station end of the platform, the dramatic profile of the glass-roofed structure raises the expectations of outgoing travellers.

If modern architects had started successfully to make inroads with large-scale schemes, many of them were also working within existing structures as they designed shop and restaurant interiors. Concealed within the shell of older buildings on the high street, they often did not have to contend with such tight planning controls. Designer shops and restaurants also depended on looking fashionable and modern for their customers. This called upon an attention to detail, which was often gem-like in effect, contained in confined spaces. Its champion in the late 1980s was Eva Jiricna, who designed a string of shops and cafés for Joseph in Kensington and Knightsbridge (1987–9). She created luminous spaces through an extensive use of glass and steel, and by employing white wall surfaces, which she treated with beeswax. The main focal point of her projects were the stairs, which combined her trademark tensile cables and glass treads in a skeleton-like intricacy.

The contrast between the two renditions of British modernism (a rather standard, dreary interpretation of the postwar International Style, and the rejuvenated modernism of the late 1980s and 90s) can be most keenly experienced at Kensington Place. In this 1987 restaurant conversion at the Notting Hill Gate end of Kensington Church Street, Wickham Associates took an unprepossessing 1960s modernist block and transformed it with a modern intervention. The main elevation was opened up to look like a factory wall with steel and glass. The new glass front and the heightened ceiling not only admit a great amount of light, but also create a sense of airiness in a restaurant that is able to seat over a hundred people.

The quest for a highly controlled perfection, most often within the parameters of a shop's interior, culminated in the late 1980s and early 1990s in the 'minimalist' style, where pared-down forms, empty surfaces, simplicity and white-on-white became extolled as virtues in themselves. One its most convincing practitioners was David Chipperfield. He worked for nine months in fashion designer Issey Miyake's office in Tokyo, before returning to London with what Nonie Nieswand has described as 'the slate, stone and wood concept of "shop as shrine" that hit the fashion retail business around 1987'.[17] The rigour with which the style was applied, particularly by John Pawson and Claudio Silvestrin, however, made it the cause of much media attention, and even ridicule. A mid-1990s TV advertisement for Imperial Leather sent up a Pawsonesque interior by suggesting that in such self-inflicted austerity even their luxury soap became an unpermitted indulgence. A more recent BBC television documentary, which was dedicated to the understanding of the 'bare' or 'minimalist' philosophy, featured potential buyers being shown around

Right Eva Jiricna, Joseph Store, Old Conran Building, London, 1988. Czech-born Eva Jiricna has developed her modernist heritage into a love of detailing. This has been expressed most keenly in the staircases that she produced during the 1980s for the designer, Joseph Ettedgui, in his West End Joseph shops. With their finely tensioned cables and glass steps, the stairs have now become something of a trademark for both the architect and the clothes designer.

Claudio Silvestrin's Riverside Apartment in Battersea in the opening sequence. Although the flat was sold at the end of the programme, the implication was that the interior design was too uncompromising to attract a buyer who would want to maintain Silvestrin's scheme.[18]

Modernizing the modern Although the minimalists certainly have a place within the history of the renaissance of 'the modern' in the 1990s, I have chosen not to focus on them here. The architects featured are those whose work has shown a particular aptitude for modernizing – whether it be in working with modern technologies or processes, like Future Systems or Fin Architects, or seeking a way to reinvent the plan of the domestic house, like Mark Guard. Formally, their work varies from the futuristic and Pop-inspired to projects that reformulate the language and form of the Modern Movement.

Fin, the architecture practice headed by Andy Martin, is responsible for some of the most fashionable new retail and restaurant spaces in Britain. Its restaurant, Mash (see page 52), has plugged into the same sci-fi feel and trend for 1970s colours and shapes that can be found in contemporary British graphics, furniture design and fashion. Such a direct translation of up-to-the-minute predilections into built form is wholly symptomatic of modernism in the 1990s, which has started to blur earlier distinctions between architecture, interior design and cultural activities. This has been facilitated in the last few years by the use of the computer, which has speeded up the design process and allowed it to become more homogenous. Martin, who earned a living designing furniture before returning to architecture, has championed the use of the computer in this way. As he has described: 'I start with a silhouette and build it into three dimensions by extruding or rotating. It makes sense because the processes used to manufacture the fittings and furniture mirror the programs we draw with.'[19]

Of all the British practices featured here, only Fin is relatively new. Future Systems, founded in 1979 by Jan Kaplicky, a Czech émigré, is a long-time favourite among students and academics. Although well known for its endless experimentation with forms, technology and ideas, the practice's work remained largely on the drawing board until the early 1990s when it started to receive commissions for built work. In 1994, Future Systems attracted a substantial amount of media attention for the Hauer-King House, with two television documentaries and a monograph devoted to it.[20] Popularly known as 'the glass house', it is a spectacular, transparent, pyramid-shaped structure in

Right David Chipperfield Architects, Issey Miyake, London, 1988. In the late 1980s/early 1990s, British minimalist architecture and interior design emerged with a new eastern or Zen emphasis. In Chipperfield's shop for Japanese fashion designer Issey Miyake, the basement level evokes the spare atmosphere of a Buddhist monk's cell. This is largely achieved through his allocation of half the floor area as empty space, which is sparsely detailed with a wooden floor, long bench and marble-effect wall.

London's Islington, built on the site of a former Georgian terrace. In 1998 the reputation of Future Systems was further consolidated with a major retrospective at the Institute of Contemporary Arts in London, while its first important public building, the NatWest Media Centre at Lord's Cricket Ground (see page 54) neared completion.

During the 1980s, such recognition would have been unthinkable. Future Systems' work, which builds on the energy and fantastic imagery of 1960s paper architecture, such as that by Archigram, was just the sort of output that was condemned by business and the establishment as unrealistic, an uncommercial architectural indulgence. This transition in Future Systems' fortunes makes its inclusion in this book doubly important. Its widespread acceptance, in the late 1990s, is indicative of the general move towards modernization. The improbable-looking, curvaceous and organic designs that Future Systems produces look computer-originated (although in fact the office has only relatively recently begun to use computers for design purposes). This makes them particularly appealing to the 'new establishment' or to commercial clients who want to align themselves with technology as a way of showing that their institution or business is 'keeping up'.[21] In addition, Future Systems' work has struck a fashionable chord, with its amorphous shapes and 'retro-futurist' feel. It is a trend that Marcus Field has perfectly summed up: 'The postwar North American look is back, and in a big way. Conversation pits, plastic and pods, packaged up and remodelled in *Wallpaper**, are the thing. If Future Systems weren't riding high on the wave, something would be wrong.'[22]

The modernity of Mark Guard's work is in a very different realm to that of Future Systems. Aesthetically it relies on the Modern Movement for its inspiration, as Guard himself concedes: 'In some respects our work is referential. We cannot claim to break new ground. Our work seeks to build on the ideas of the Modern Movement and seek solutions that improve the quality of life.'[23] It is Guard's preoccupation with the social aspect of housing, however, that makes his work particularly important. In this sense, he is a true modernizer as he seeks to meet the demands of life in the 1990s in a way that is redolent of the Modern Movement. As he puts it himself: 'Contemporary architecture seems devoid of social comment … with such a vacuum of thought, the early work of Corbusier, Schindler, Neutra, Rietveld and so on provides an interesting basis on which to build for the future.'[24] Although most of his projects are refurbishments or renovations (which is partly due to the scarcity of land in London, where he works) he has sought to question to its fundamentals the conventional use of domestic space. In his houses at Kensal Rise and Deptford, the existing structures

1 For a full discussion of the perceived failure of modernism in Britain see Adrian Forty, 'Being or Nothingness: Private Experience and Public Architecture in Post-War Britain', *Architectural History* 38, 1995, pp25–35.

2 Lionel Esher, *A Broken Wave: The Rebuilding of England 1940–1980* (London), 1981, p285.

3 For further discussion of Venturi and Jencks see Jayne Merkel's essay, 'Modernism Redux', p64 .

4 Tom Wolfe, *From Bauhaus to Our House*, Picador (London), 1993, p6. Initially published as a series of articles in *Harper's* (New York) in the summer of 1981, the book was first published in Great Britain in 1982 by Johnathan Cape.

5 For a full description of Paternoster Square see Maureen Gourlay, 'Paternoster Square and St Paul's: an Architectural Dilemma', MSc thesis for the Bartlett, University College, London, 1997.

6 Forty, 'Being or Nothingness', p27.

7 Miles Glendinning and Stefan Muthesius, *Tower Block: Modern Public Housing in England, Scotland, Wales and Northern Ireland*, Yale University Press (London), 1994, p313.

8 See Charles Jenning, 'Modern Manner', *Space, The Guardian*, 20 March 1998, pp10–13.

9 Charles Jencks and Karl Kropf (eds), *Theories and Manifestoes of Contemporary Architecture*, Academy Editions (London), 1997, p253. First published in Frank Russell (ed.), *Architectural Monographs: Richard Rogers + Architects*, Academy Editions (London), 1985.

10 Jencks and Kropf (eds), *Theories and Manifestoes*, p248. First published in *Architectural Design* vol XLV, no 5, 1975.

11 Michael Sorkin, *The Exquisite Corpse*, Verso (London & New York), 1991, p132.

12 Colin Rowe, 'James Stirling: A Highly Personal and Very Disjointed Memoir', Peter Arnell and Ted Bickford, *James Stirling: Buildings and Projects*, The Architectural Press (London), 1984, pp10–27.

13 Ibid, p16.

14 Kenneth Frampton, *Modern Architecture: A Critical History*, Thames and Hudson (London), third edition, 1992, p267.

become nothing more than a shell, accommodating homes that completely revise the traditional plan of the family house. Thus they meet more closely the needs and desires of their clients. Likewise the Transformable Apartment, in Soho, is an essay in urban housing, seeking to create the flexibility and economy demanded by modern living.

Like Mark Guard, who did his apprenticeship among the British modern establishment of Richard Rogers, Rick Mather and Eva Jiricna, Seth Stein worked for Rogers and Sir Norman Foster before setting up his own practice in the late 1980s. He displays a similar confidence and fine-tuning in his use of materials, and an insistence on the importance of light: both Guard and Stein use glass floors/ceilings to introduce light from above into the lower levels (see Guard's House Refurbishment in Kensal Rise and Stein's Pied-à-terre in Knightsbridge, pages 56 and 62). Stein's Pied-à-terre also shows a modern – and distinctly British – ingenuity. The addition of a car lift would be entirely Heath Robinson if it was not executed with such a sophisticated exuberance. The lift epitomizes the sense of modish playfulness that is so current in British architecture today, and which to a certain extent can be regarded as an adverse reaction to the uncompromising minimalism of the early 1990s.

The diversity of the work shown on the following pages, all produced by British architects in the late 1990s, might well beg the question: what, then, is modernism today? For in the process of reviving modernism, which has involved shedding the dogma of the postwar International Style, architects have also shrugged off its uniting ideology and formal characteristics. Modernism is now a certain attitude, more than anything else. Taking their cue from Richard Rogers, the next generation of architects are endlessly trying 'to expand [the Modern Movement's] approach to meet constantly changing needs' (see page 21). While these architects might not be advocating the sort of social ideology that held sway in the postwar years, they are nevertheless insisting on the relevance of technical innovation and forward-thinking solutions. One of the most salient features of current design is the type of futuristic imaging inherited from Archigram and the high-tech movement. Internationally, the British also distinguish themselves with their craftsmanship and attention to detail, which has once again been passed on from the high-tech architects to practitioners such as Seth Stein and Mark Guard. It transpires that the so-called 'death of modernism' in Britain in the 1980s was no more than a near-death experience, in which the high-tech architects coaxed it back to life for a younger generation of designers in the 1990s.

15 Samantha Hardingham, *England: A Guide to Recent Architecture*, Ellipsis (London), 1995, p11.

16 Liz Jobey, 'The Grand Designer', *The Guardian Weekend*, 27 June 1998, p13. In this article on Sir Norman Foster, Jobey also makes the point that for the first time at the end of the 1990s, Foster is building all over the UK: projects included a new concert hall in Gateshead, the British Museum, Wembley Stadium and Botanical Gardens in Wales.

17 Nonie Niesewand, 'Art and Craft', *Vogue*, April 1998, p208.

18 'Bare', Modern Times, BBC Television, first shown on 11 March 1998. (Series editor, Stephen Lambert; producer, Belinda Allen; director, Rebecca Frayn.)

19 Liz Farrelly, 'Tales of the Unexpected', *Blueprint*, April 1988, p22.

20 'House of Glass', Without Walls, Channel 4, 1994; 'Glass House' Building Sites, BBC 2; and Martin Pawley, *Hauer-King House*, Architecture in Detail, Phaidon (London), 1997.

21 Despite the conservative practices at Lord's (women were only permitted entry into the clubhouse in 1998) the club has a tradition of innovative design, having commissioned the Mound Stand in 1985 from Michael Hopkins & Partners. Another example of members of the establishment 'keeping up' is the House in Wales pp54–5, designed for a Labour MP.

22 Marcus Field, 'Tomorrow's World', *Blueprint* (London), March 1998, p26.

23 Mark Guard's response to some questions put to him by the author on 5 May 1998.

24 Ibid.

A venue for hip chicks and understated trainer-clad lads working in London's media land, Mash is situated in Great Portland Street among a string of bargain fashion retail shops, just the other side of Oxford Street from Soho. A great airy space, which seats 145 on well-spaced tables divided between the ground floor and mezzanine levels, it poses as a cross between a 1970s airport lounge and a 1960s sc-fi TV show. On the street, the partition of the two floors is made apparent by tall plate-glass windows cut into the existing facade. The diner is welcomed in a white foyer parallel to the pavement, which contains a take-away counter on the left and a newspaper kiosk on the right, inserted into the wall with Fin's trademark globular form. Above the entrance to the ground-floor dining room, Murray Partridge's installation *Love Machine* – which takes the form of an arrivals/departures board – greets the visitor with its quirky messages and catches the attention of curious passers-by.

Unlike Manchester's Mash & Air, the flagship restaurant designed by Fin's Andy Martin with fellow expat antipodean Marc Newson, Mash is located within an existing structure. This has been most successfully handled at the front of the restaurant, where a luminous white foyer has been created out of the area between the original glass-fronted street facade and a second elevation in the interior.

The treatment of the ground-floor dining-room space is more cosmetic than architectural; it has to rely for its plastic effect on the walls – which sweep down in a curve at the floor – and further globular hatch inserts. The lounge bar to the right dazzles with a kitsch photo-mural that has all the colour subtlety of an episode of 'Hawaii Five O'. Fitted out with beige sofas, pouffe cushions and chrome tables, it encapsulates the contemporary mood – magazines stage photo shoots here and TV crews use it as a backdrop for interviews. The upstairs restaurant, which is accessed by an undulating staircase covered in customized pebble-dash, has the advantage of being a lighter space, more immediately open to the window facade.

The *pièce de résistance* of this sophisticated eatery, however, is the toilets. The joke seems to be on the men. In the Gents', the magnifying reflective urinals give the diner an unrealistic image of himself. In the Ladies', small screens above a mirrored trough sink create a direct video link with the Gents', revealing a view of their basins. By introducing such devices and engaging in a sophisticated quirky chic – curvy sci-fi forms and 1970s styling – Fin has not only created an upbeat atmosphere, but has also been confident enough to suggest that Mash diners should be doing what people do best when they go out: enjoying themselves.

Fin Architects
Mash
London, 1998

Opposite above Murray Partridge's arrivals and departures board-style installation, *Love Machine*, in the restaurant foyer. **Opposite below** The take-away food counter in Mash's foyer, which caters for the large number of office workers in the vicinity. **Left** One of the globular niches that are a recurrent feature in the restaurant. **Above** The lounge bar, which is to the right of the ground-floor restaurant, featuring John Currin's technicolour kitsch photo-mural and Fin's custom-made 1970s airport-style seating.

Left Computer-simulated image of the NatWest Media Centre in place at Lord's. The centre, which has been built to accommodate the press and other media staff, recasts the cricket club in a futuristic light. **Below right** Computer rendering of House in Pembrokeshire, showing the building emerging from the ground like a natural crater in a rugged landscape. **Below left** Model of the prefabricated classroom designed for Hallfield School, which with its glazed form introduces a new transparency into prefab classroom design.

Future Systems
NatWest Media Centre
Lord's Cricket Ground, London
due for completion late 1998

House in Pembrokeshire
Wales, 1998

Hallfield School
Competition Design
London, 1996

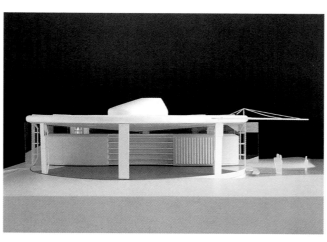

1 Martin Pawley, *Future Systems*, catalogue for exhibition at the Institute of Contemporary Arts, London, 1998.
2 Future Systems' scheme was to have cost £1.7 million. Despite optimistic murmurings from the Lottery Commission, the application was disqualified for being educational. See Jonathan Glancey, 'It Looks like a Lemon Grater Crossed with a Spaceship … And Kids love it', *The Guardian*, 23 February 1998, pp10–11.

NatWest Media Centre

The Media Centre at Lord's realizes the ultimate yearnings of the Modern Movement, for an architecture that is aeronautical or machine-like. It is one of the first buildings to adopt, wholesale, construction methods developed by the transport industries: it is to be built for the most part by a boatyard rather than the building industry. The seamless oval shell of the centre is being constructed and fitted out off-site in a boatyard in Falmouth, using the latest advances in boat-building technology. To Future Systems, the Media Centre's importance lies in it being 'the first all-aluminium semi-monocoque building in the world',[1] referring to the aircraft or vehicle structure whose aerodynamic form has a chassis integral with the body. Despite being prefabricated and taking a futuristic, curvaceous form, the centre has been carefully conceived to echo the sweep of the existing cricket ground. Once in use by the world's media it will appear as a huge eye or screen looking over the grounds.

House in Pembrokeshire

This house embraces what have traditionally been regarded as two unreconcilable aims: absolute modernity, and an uncompromising respect for nature. Located on a cliff face in the Pembrokeshire National Park, it takes its inspiration from its dramatic site and the wild beauty of the landscape. Futuristic and bunker-like, the house is camouflaged with turf so that it merges with the existing landscape of rugged grass. (It is only at the surface of the earth that it emerges as a elliptical glass eye viewing the coastline.) There are no marked-out boundary lines, nor is there a plotted garden. A similarly informal approach has been adopted for the interior. The main living area is centred around an open log fire with two freestanding, prefabricated pods accommodating the kitchen and bathroom. Commissioned by a Labour MP, the house is a sure sign of the practice's endorsement by the new establishment. It also, quite inadvertently, expresses the preoccupations of present politicians , reconciling environmental concerns with modernizing tendencies.

Hallfield School Competition Design

During the 1980s and 1990s, the lack of money available for schools and other state-funded institutions in Britain has meant that architects have had little opportunity to re-examine the typologies of public buildings which were first explored by postwar designers, often working for local government. Future Systems' designs for prefabricated pavilions at Hallfield School display not only a keen awareness of the needs of the contemporary primary school and its pupils, but also a sensitivity to the original building, completed by Sir Denys Lasdun in 1954. The project was the winning entry for a competition held by Hallfield's governors, and judged by Lasdun and Richard Rogers, in an attempt at a bid to secure funding from the National Lottery for much-needed extra classroom space.[2] Future Systems' solution was to propose planting six new pavilions in the landscaped gardens. This linked back to Lasdun's motif of an unfurling leaf, which he used to describe his concept of the school. Each pavilion would have been like a new growth on an existing stem. By proposing prefabricated units, Future Systems was exploring the possibilities of a generic design for other schools and nurseries up and down the country. Circular, top-lit and transparent, with adequate backing they could be as ubiquitous, in the future, as the Clasp System of school building developed in the 1950s.

When David Hare chose to set his play *Skylight* in an inner London suburb that symbolized the ordinariness of someone's life, he chose Kensal Rise. Although just north of Notting Hill, the area has not undergone the middle-class gentrification of its neighbour. Made up of surprisingly quiet streets of late Victorian and early twentieth-century houses, it is the kind of place where people wash their cars on a Sunday. It is also the sort of place in which most people in Britain live – making it fertile ground for architectural exploration. For despite the changes in modern living patterns, needs and desires, few suburban houses have undergone fundamental changes since they were built. Most simply undergo a process of evolution and addition, such as an extra porch, window or extension out the back.

Mark Guard's response to his clients' request to design them a new home was both practical and uncompromising. By advising them to buy a house that was in need of complete renovation, he was able to cost the refurbishment according to the estimated price that the house would reach on the market once renovated. The poor condition of the house gave him the additional leeway to radically question its conventional organization: 'The problem with the layout of the traditional Victorian terrace is that the extended part at the back cuts off the ground floor from light and from the garden,' says Guard.

'Turn it upside-down and you get more light into the living spaces where you want it.'"

This is what he did. Inverting the traditional plan of an English suburban house, Guard opened up the first floor to accommodate the kitchen, dining room and living room, while adding a second staircase to give access to the garden and conservatory below. This solution had the added benefit of being cheaper than making structural changes to the ground floor.

Below, the bedrooms and bathrooms are situated in what used to be the main living space. The front ground-floor bedroom is open to the hallway and is used as a study, with the possibility of converting it into a third bedroom. The rest of the ground floor is planned as 'transformable space'. Depending on which doors are open, the master bedroom can have an en-suite dressing area and one or two bathrooms, or the back guest room can have the shower room en-suite. Alternatively, a laundry room can be created from the bathroom area.

Downstairs, a sense of openness is maintained as light (from a first-floor rooflight) enters via a glass ceiling in the dressing area. A double-height conservatory behind the new rear elevation also opens up the guest room (or 'den'), and the upstairs kitchen–living room, to the garden. In the breakfast area a clear glass balustrade allows views down to the deck below.

Mark Guard
House Refurbishment
in Kensal Rise
London, 1994

1 Quoted in David Redhead, 'Let there
  be Light', *Independent* magazine,
  16 September 1995, p30.

Opposite Double-height glass elevation at the back of the house. **Above left** Detail of clear glass balustrade on the first floor. **Above right** View of upstairs living area with main stairs from the front door. **Far left** The kitchen, situated in the middle of the first floor between the main living–dining space and the breakfast area. **Left** The horizontal breakfast bar, shown here, continues into the kitchen, where it becomes the main counter, and then through to the living room, where the change in level transforms it into a low coffee table.

This house creates a modernist haven from the rigours of daily life within a run-down area of southeast London, Deptford, which is dominated by council estates. Encased in a nineteenth-century shell, which was previously a two-storey brick coach house, the building focuses on a double-height internal garden, which its clients refer to as a garden of remembrance.[1] By reorienting the house and determining its views, a further step was taken to control its environment: the windows on the west side of the coach house facing the courtyard were bricked up to avoid being overlooked by neighbouring houses, and a large window on the first-floor east side of the coach house was created to take advantage of the view towards Nicholas Hawksmoor's St Paul's church and Greenwich in the distance.

As with Guard's house in Kensal Rise, the living room and kitchen are on the first floor and the bedrooms and studios on the ground floor. This has the advantage of bringing light into the kitchen and living room through the exterior east side. It is, however, the inclusion of the garden within the house that makes the most radical break with traditional uses of domestic space. The entrance courtyard on one side of the coach house, and the secluded walled garden on the other, were both accommodated in the new scheme by removing the rudimentary roofs of the existing building. Outside and inside space not only connect but also become blurred. The entire east (garden-side) wall of the coach house is made up of double-glazed sliding glass doors, which can be drawn back on both upper and lower levels. An entrance axis through the house from the courtyard further encourages occupants or visitors towards the garden. The axis is emphasized visually by a linear pond and a new door in the walled garden, which can be used as a separate entrance for the garden studio on the ground floor. Freestanding concrete pillars define the spaces while also supporting the steel beams which are necessary to brace the existing walls and support the new sliding walls.

The spare, modernist detailing reinforces the overall impression of an early twentieth-century Californian house. At ground level the floors are of raw concrete, looking like a smooth version of the gravel in the garden. Internal walls are of white plaster, and in the kitchen the usual stainless steel fittings have been avoided. This minimalism perfectly suits the function of the house and the lifestyle of the owners, who use it to display their collection of modern furniture to best advantage.

Mark Guard
New House in Deptford
London, 1995

1 See 'Bare', Modern Lives, BBC Television. The suggestion in the programme was that the garden was created to remember friends who had died of a modern disease.

Opposite above View from the internal garden into the ground-floor bedroom. **Opposite below** The kitchen, situated on the first floor of the coach house. **Above** At the end of the garden is a ground-floor studio and steps leading up to a roof terrace. In front of the studio is the linear pond that flanks the path, which is designed to draw visitors out of the house. **Right** Cross section showing the transformation of the coach house, with garage space on either side, into a house with a garden to the left and entrance courtyard to the right.

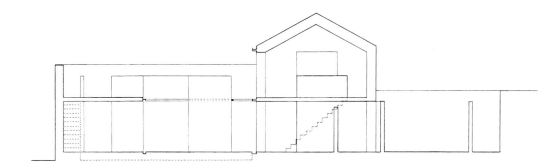

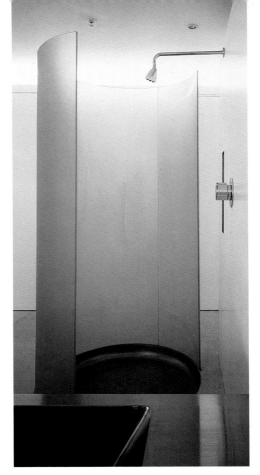

This apartment is a direct response to changing living patterns. Although most of Britain's housing stock caters for the static model of a family unit with 2.2 children, many people now need more flexible homes. Today, far more people live alone than did so thirty years ago; at the same time they require the space to accommodate an extra person from time to time, be it a partner, guest or child.' The situation is exacerbated by the high premium that land commands, especially in the inner cities, which makes it no longer viable for single people or couples to occupy whole family houses.

Located in Soho, in the heart of London's West End, this apartment explores the ways that flexible use can maximize available space. Although its total area is only 90 square metres (970 square feet), the apartment can provide one or two bedrooms; alternatively it can be used as one big living space. This is achieved by accommodating the master bedroom and guest room in two freestanding boxes, and the cloakroom in a third. These three boxes enclose the bathroom, where the bath is set into a 6-metre (20-foot) steel table. The bath's Privalite glass surround can be switched from opaque to clear, giving a view from the bath and also providing a visual focus to the apartment when the bedroom partitions are folded away.

To achieve a simple neutrality, the space is painted white and is detailed sparely. Much of the floor area is given over to cupboards, as ample storage is essential to an economical and uncluttered use of space. The kitchen, laundry, dressing table, wardrobes, washbasin and television and hi-fi are all concealed by one long row of doors, as are three work areas, a washing-up unit, a cooking area and a coffee/drinks bar. The flat has a limestone floor throughout that is visually unifying, and provides a durable surface for both living and working.

Mark Guard
Transformable Loft
Apartment in Soho
London, 1996

1 Mark Guard Architects supports this finding with the following statistics: between 1961 and 1991, the proportion of one-person households in the UK rose from 12 to 36 per cent. In the same period, the proportion of households comprising only one person or couples without children has risen to 62 per cent. The figures are even more pronounced in inner-city areas.

Opposite above The shower, with its curved surround, creates part of a freestanding sculptural bathroom.
Opposite below The long stainless-steel bench, which was an important feature of the Kensal Rise House, reappears here as a dining/study table.
Above The main living space, showing the freestanding box which houses the bathroom. Above the bench is the bath's Privalite glass screen. **Right** The kitchen work areas revealed from behind cupboard doors to show, left to right, sections for coffee/drinks, cooking and washing up.

Structured around a hydraulic lift with two car decks, this modern mews house brings the motor car and occupier into a proximity that could only have previously been dreamt of in a 1960s futuristic fantasy. It provides the ultimate flexible domestic space for a young couple who wanted to accommodate their collection of vintage and special edition cars within their own habitat. The two car decks, situated at the main living level (below ground) and at street level, can be lowered to store two vehicles; when raised the decks allow space for a translucent-ceilinged basement living room, four steps down from the adjoining dining room.

Representing a hip, expensive chic, the house seems to belong to the virtual world of celluloid. It is difficult to picture it being occupied on a day-to-day basis by anyone other than a character from the movies, delivering cars or guests up and down the moving floors with dry martini in hand. Its improbability advances the image of futuristic modernity, which is further exaggerated by its exclusive location in Knightsbridge and its fine detailing. The juxtaposition of limestone flooring, specially treated glass and a hydraulic lift with the aesthetics of an aircraft carrier heighten the effect. It has the cool spareness and austerity of a contemporary art gallery in which single items of furniture or vintage cars are the venerated objects on display.

The sophistication of the completed pied-à-terre, however, belies the problematic, and thoroughly typical, modern urban conditions in which the house was built. The house was wrought out of a tiny site, 4.5 metres (15 feet) wide by 8.5 metres (28 feet) long, at the end of an existing mews. The exterior was also subject to planning restrictions: the front and rear elevations were required to be in line with the adjacent row of existing houses, which allowed it to have a depth of no more than 5 metres (16½ feet). In addition to this, the facade was required to replicate the original terrace.

The architects responded to the restrictions of the brief by excavating the site to a depth of 3.5 metres (11½ feet) and digging a shaft of 7 metres (23 feet) to accommodate the hydraulic lift. This not only allowed them to create additional space, in the form of a basement living room, when the lift is raised, but also to introduce light into the house's depths: the transparent acrylic panels of the deck's ceiling allow a clear upwards view through the house. Light also penetrates through the main sandblasted glass floor and stairs, and the transparent lower lift deck, via a glass panel to the rear courtyard and a strip of roof lights along the rear boundary. In addition, the translucent stairs, which rise in straight flights through the house, lead the eye skywards to a window capturing a square of blue.

Seth Stein Architects
Pied-à-terre in Knightsbridge
London, 1997

Opposite View of the back of the house, showing the limited site and the architect's economical use of space. The glass strip roof lights, in the foreground, and the opaque glass panel in the rear wall, help to maximize the amount of light entering the basement and ground floor. **Above** The basement dining area with the car deck lowered, shutting off the living area. **Right** The basement kitchen looking up towards the sandblasted glass stairs. **Far right** The basement living room which is created when the lift is raised.

Modern architecture is back.
And in the US it is back most visibly in the very place where it was first introduced:
MoMA (the Museum of Modern Art) in New York.
After a carefully watched, well-publicized two-year search,
the museum selected for its addition a quiet, light-filled, white-walled, rectilinear design
by the Japanese architect Yoshio Taniguchi. To the untried eye at least, it looks not unlike the original galleries that
Philip Goodwin and Edward Durrell Stone built for the museum in 1939.
The addition, however, does not represent a return to that kind of International Style architecture; instead it presents a de-radicalized, aestheticized, late twentieth-century form of modernism that respects historic architecture and absorbs it, rather than rejecting its premises and charting a completely new course.

The Taniguchi scheme belongs to the body of self-consciously modern recent architectural work that has largely replaced the post-modern revivalism that dominated the US architectural scene in the late 1970s and 1980s, especially in and around New York.' All the semi-finalists — Wiel Arets, Jacques Herzog and Pierre de Meuron, Steven Holl, Toyo Ito, Rem Koolhaas, Dominique Perrault, Taniguchi, Bernard Tschumi, Rafael Viñoly, Tod Williams and Billie Tsien — work in this quiet, absorptive modern mode, although the differences in their work are almost as great as the commonalties. At least that is how it seems in the 1990s when the existence of several artistic directions at once is presumed, even at the museum that has been responsible for codifying one style after another.

It was, after all, only after MoMA held its major exhibition entitled 'Modern Architects', in 1932, that the stranglehold that Beaux-Arts classicism held upon the American architectural establishment began to relax, though Frank Lloyd Wright had been creating masterful, pioneering, indigenous modern buildings for forty years. The show accomplished exactly what the two young architectural historians who organized it, Henry Russell Hitchcock and Philip Johnson (who not yet become an architect), had intended. They had discovered the new European modern architecture on a trip to Europe in 1930 and set out with missionary zeal to bring it home, first organizing a Salon des Refusés for modern architects who had been excluded from the prestigious annual Architectural League exhibition, then convincing their friend Alfred Barr, the director of the fledging MoMA, to do a major show, and writing a book on the work they admired most.[2] The MoMA exhibition, which was put together by a museum committee and travelled throughout the US, was more comprehensive than

Modernism Redux   *Jayne Merkel*

New York in the 1990s

the book. It included Frank Lloyd Wright, and a section on housing curated by Lewis Mumford. But the book, *The International Style: Architecture Since 1922*, which omitted both, had a far more lasting effect on the type of modern architecture that would be built in the US, the way it would be conceived (as a style rather than a social movement), and the fact that it came to be associated with modern art, European influence and a cultural elite.[3]

Since 'modern architecture' had been defined by Hitchcock and Johnson as 'International Style', the first buildings in New York to be considered modern were ones designed by European émigrés or, like the MoMA itself, by Americans who had adopted the International Style. These included Joseph Urban's New School for Social Research of 1930 (an entire institution founded by refugees from Hitler's Germany); William Lescaze's townhouse on East 48th Street of 1934; and MoMA's own building on West 53rd Street. All were devoted to high culture. Although a few low-cost housing projects began to be built in the US under government auspices in the 1930s, most were made of traditional red brick with minimal concern for style. Some, however, did adopt Le Corbusier's 'tower in the park' planning model.

The triumph of the International Style really became apparent after the end of the Second World War. Building was now resumed on a large scale. The Art Deco and Moderne styles that had dominated commercial and residential building in the 1920s and 30s, especially in New York, were nowhere to be found. Flat roofs replaced decorative pinnacles. Ornamentation disappeared from facades. Glass doors and window walls replaced the elaborate portals and framed windows that had once pierced heavy masonry facades, usually in brick with stone or terracotta trim. Glass and steel appeared as exterior building materials, most noticeably in the United Nations Headquarters by Wallace K Harrison and an international team of architects (including Le Corbusier, Oscar Niemeyer and Sven Markelius) of 1947–53; Lever House by Gordon Bunshaft of Skidmore, Owings & Merrill (1952); and the Seagram Building across the street from it at Park Avenue and 53rd Street (1958) by Mies van der Rohe with Philip Johnson, who by now had become an architect.

Soon, every new building had a plain facade, flat roof, undemarcated entry, visible structural skeleton and flat surfaces. A zoning bonus for the creation of a plaza (established to compensate for the fact that Seagram's had been taxed even for the part of the lot retained as open space) led to whole blocks lined with empty plazas, especially on New York's Sixth Avenue.[4] In the hands of lesser architects than Mies and Bunshaft, as most were, the style which required perfect

Previous page Bart Voorsanger, Garden Court, Pierpont Morgan Library, New York, 1990. Prominently positioned on Manhattan's Madison Avenue, Voorsanger's Garden Court epitomizes the modern reductionist solution to building in a high-profile historic context. It provides a neutral, clean glass and steel palimpsest to its neighbours on either side: McKim, Mead & White's original Pierpont Morgan Library and an Italianate brownstone from the 1850s.

proportions, careful detailing and high-quality materials rapidly deteriorated into bland, characterless boxes without the ornamentation that had relieved bad traditional buildings. Larger size and scale further dehumanized modern buildings. SOM's hulking 60-storey, 170,000-square-metre (1,820,000-square-foot) One Chase Manhattan Bank Plaza of 1955–60, for example, dwarfed most of the nearby skyscrapers, and its vast superblock site cut a big chunk out of the old Wall Street canyons.

In the US, this style was largely confined to commercial, industrial and institutional buildings. Most Americans continued to live in detached, single-family houses, largely hand-built – without architects – employing a variety of synthetic materials in confused versions of traditional styles. The situation continues to this day. Rather than build modern housing blocks, the federal government provides subsidies in the form of loan programmes and tax incentives for individual home ownership. The urban poor live in publicly supported housing, while in the country, those on low incomes live in privately owned trailers with traditional trim. Americans have often tended to reject a modern vocabulary for buildings they cared deeply about, such as churches and colleges. Modernism never meant anything more to them than efficiency, modernity (in a cold, rootless sense), and economy.

Only in New York was the new housing of the majority of the middle and upper classes modern and multi-family. Even here, modern high-rise private housing was largely confined to the city centre – Manhattan – and a few prime neighbourhoods in Brooklyn, Queens and the Bronx. The new blank-walled Manhattan apartment buildings that went up in the 1950s and 60s were often built of white brick to approximate (rather poorly) the stucco or concrete of the early European International Style. Many had balconies – narrow, dark and soon soot-filled – intended to recall Corbusian roof gardens. Some had shops at the base – another adaptation of European precedent as well as a concession to continually rising Manhattan land values and, later, as a response to urban design theory that believed (rightly) that retail activity created more street life.

Post-modernism and historicism This theory stemmed mainly from the observations of a maverick architectural journalist, Jane Jacobs, whose *Death and Life of Great American Cities* argued that old-fashioned city blocks, such as those in New York's Greenwich Village where she lived, were safer and more sociable than the Corbusian planning favoured by modern theorists and employed at government housing projects. Old neighbourhoods certainly functioned better, but that may have been partly because so many of the residents in public housing were socially disadvantaged.[5] Still, the failures of the housing projects were used as evidence that modern architecture itself was the culprit, and that it needed to be replaced with the new products of what came to be called the 'post-modern' movement. Charles Jencks' influential book, *The Language of Post-Modern Architecture,* began: 'Happily, we can date the death of modern architecture to a precise moment in time … Modern Architecture died in St Louis, Missouri on July 15, 1972 at 3:32 pm (or thereabouts) when the infamous Pruitt-Igoe scheme, or rather several of its slab blocks, were given the final coup de grâce by dynamite.' The project, designed by Minoru Yamasaki in 1952–5, had indeed been vandalized by its inhabitants, but not simply because of its design.

Jencks' book was one of several that heralded the advent of post-modernism. A very different kind of critique than Jacobs', it was more a polemic for symbolism in architecture than an analysis of modernism's weaknesses. Robert Venturi's earlier, more scholarly and theoretical *Complexity and Contradiction in Architecture* of 1966, which was published by MoMA as the first (and only) of its 'Papers on Architecture' series, contained a more sustained critique of modernism's single-minded approach. In order to make this critique, however, Venturi had to define modern architecture in the narrow terms of Hitchcock and Johnson's International Style rather than in a more inclusive way that would have considered the work of Wright, Aalto, Louis Kahn and the many other architects whose work contained the complexity – if not the overt symbolism – that Venturi recommended. The book made a considerable impact, especially in the prestigious architecture schools of the New York region, but Jencks' easier-to-read, livelier, more pictorial and popular book had more widespread influence.

Another factor contributing to the growth of the post-modern movement was the increasing popularity of historic preservation in the US – a land where hitherto the new had almost always been considered preferable to the old. The Urban Renewal 'slum clearance' programme, initiated after the Second World War, had created new frontiers by demolishing whole parts of cities and erecting sanitary new Voisin Plan-style housing towers. But since government leaders were more zealous about getting rid of the poor than helping them relocate, many low-income communities dispersed. By the end of the 1950s many US cities, although untouched by war, were more visibily changed than their European counterparts that had been levelled by bombing and rebuilt. Urban renewal areas frequently became wastelands because of excessive scale, lack of street life, and the amount of land devoted to the automobile.

In comparison with redesigned ones, old neighbourhoods now began to look appealing, and their relative rarity made them as desirable as new buildings had once been. Historic preservation eventually outstripped any of the earlier architectural styles in popularity, for it offered the comfort of the familiar, a sense of roots that appealed to transient Americans, and traditional natural materials at a time when naturalness was gaining favour in food, dress, make-up and fabrics. In New York City, the demolition of Pennsylvania Station (a monumental work by McKim, Mead & White based on the Baths of Caracalla in Rome) in 1963 led, two years later, to the establishment of a law to protect historic treasures. A National Historic Preservation Act came into effect in 1966, and the Federal Tax Reform Act of 1981 provided financial incentives for preservation. While the landmarks movement in America remains underfunded compared to those in Europe, it represents a sea-change in the US.

The energy crisis of 1974, too, contributed to the reappearance of historic elements in architecture. A limited supply of energy made people realize how wasteful thin-skinned, glass-walled buildings with inoperable windows were; at the same time, new research showed how efficient were many of the discredited historic features, such as steep roofs in rainy areas, and small windows with heavy curtains in cold climes. Ideas that had been advanced years earlier by James Marston Fitch in *American Building: The Environmental Forces that Shaped It* (originally published in 1947 and reissued in 1972) finally caught on. Fitch had an impact in other ways too. A modern architect and a preservationist, he founded a training programme for historic preservation at Columbia University.[6] Here his students identified and developed plans for a number of the city's under-used old neighbourhoods, such as the cast-iron, nineteenth-century industrial district of SoHo where artists were beginning to move into spacious, inexpensive lofts and were discovering high-ceilinged spaces, Corinthian capitals, ornamental window frames and decorative cornices.

These spaces provided ideal environments for contemporary art (which itself was often very stark); better, in fact, than low-ceilinged, open-plan modern apartments, which no longer seemed new and exciting. As time went on, traditional New York apartment houses of the 1900s, 1910s and 1920s came to appear 'historic' and, thus, more interesting and stylish than their modern (post-war) equivalents.

In the 1970s and 80s, the new 'post-modern' architecture – a form of architecture which resembled the old – swept the US. Even MoMA picked up on the renewed interest in drawing and the primacy of the plan, holding an exhibition entitled 'Architecture of the Ecole des Beaux-Arts' in

1975–6. But post-modernism emerged when so much building was taking place that there was little time to reflect on the new architectural language and how it might be adapted to contemporary materials, construction techniques and building programmes. A large body of mediocre post-modern work soon led to disillusionment, in the same way that poor modern buildings had. And the appetite for change created a search for ever newer trends.

Modern survivals and revivals It was thus that neo-modernism moved easily into the foreground. The 'modern' architects who had remained most prominently in the limelight through the heyday of post-modern revivalism had always shared their contemporaries' interests in history and aesthetics, according to the book that launched the careers of Peter Eisenman, Michael Graves, Charles Gwathmey, John Hejduk and Richard Meier after an exhibition at MoMA in 1969. In *Five Architects* (1972), Kenneth Frampton discussed their debts to Le Corbusier, and Colin Rowe pointed out that their work, unlike the early European modern architecture it resembled, had never been part of a social programme, though in fact Eisenman and Graves had recently done an urban design proposal for Harlem (together) and Richard Meier had built a fine moderate-income apartment building for artists in 1967 and would design a public housing project in the Bronx a decade later. Graves soon abandoned the Corbusian idiom of his early years for an expressionistic, almost anguished, personal version of post-modern classicism around 1976. But Meier and Gwathmey (who practices with Robert Siegel at Gwathmey Siegel and Associates Architects) continued to work in a manner that resembled Le Corbusier's early work. They made their smooth white walls of wood and enlarged the glazed surfaces, but continued to use the flat roofs and volumetric spaces penetrated by ramps and staircases. The spatial manipulations, play of light, and craftsmanship in both architects' work became increasingly sophisticated, complex and original over the years as they received opportunities to design big-budget museums, campus buildings and gargantuan houses.

      Hejduk built very little. He explored architectural ideas largely in drawings and as dean of architecture at the Cooper Union Foundation for Art and Science. However, in 1975, he renovated the school's 1859 Foundation Building, a hulk of brownstone with Italianate trim and the oldest extant steel-framed structure in America. He gutted the interior – leaving only a charming multi-colonnaded underground auditorium where Abraham Lincoln once spoke – filling an existing cylindrical shaft with a gigantic circular elevator surrounded by a staircase connecting studios and exhibition spaces

Right John Hejduk, Renovation of 1859 Foundation Building, Cooper Union Foundation for Art and Science, New York, 1975. In the mid 1970s, Hejduk foretold the recent tendency to create crisp geometric interiors within historic structures. He gutted the inside of this tall, arcaded, steel-framed brownstone pile and partitioned the new spaces with a complex collection of cut-out walls, linking all seven floors with a circular elevator shaft and a well of assertive open space.

on seven levels. The redesign, which turned the building into a reverse doughnut shape, still looks fresh. It is one of the masterpieces of modern design within an existing structure.

Eisenman spent the first half of his career primarily as an educator and architectural impresario, designing mainly small theoretical houses based on complex abstract structural grids.[7] But after he won a competition for the Wexner Center for the Visual Arts at the Ohio State University in 1983 (with Jaquelin Robertson, who was his partner for a short period), he began to undertake a series of public buildings. Like his earlier theoretical projects each of these buildings was inspired by ideas from other disciplines, such as semiotics, structuralism, deconstruction and folding theory. The Wexner Center presses into a non-existent site between two bland modern buildings, imposes the grid of the city plan on that of the campus plan (which is a few degrees askew), contains a recon-structed fragment of a demolished castellated armoury, and creates an interior pathway from one part of the campus to another through the art galleries; all of this while tilting, showing glimpses of spaces beyond, and more or less accommodating the complex requirements of the brief. Although Eisenman's intellectual energy is his most salient quality, his built works have a cool, eerie beauty and create a consciousness of architecture. Although none of these architects' works resembles histori-cal post-modernism, each contains complicated forms, colour, and varied shapes. Like those of other ambitious modern East Coast architects, they are complex and frequently contradictory.

A similar infusion of forms occurred in Los Angeles, although it was one of the few places in the US where historical pastiche failed to make significant inroads. Here, the seminal influ-ence was Frank Gehry, who began introducing polygonal forms, unbalanced compositions and indus-trial materials into the classic modern vocabulary he had been developing for a decade and a half in dozens of institutional and commercial buildings. In 1978 he renovated his own house, a small pink bungalow, by adding corrugated aluminum siding, a chain-link balcony, a cube window that seemed to be slipping out of its frame, a blacktop (asphalt) kitchen floor and other elements that made it look like a construction site gone mad. At the time, the project looked so radical that for a while it drove all his clients away. In the 1980s Gehry went even further, although with more refinement, and started using dramatic convoluted shapes, titanium skin and pulsating volumes – a language that reached its highest expression at the spectacular Guggenheim Museum in Bilbao, Spain (1997).

The standard of quality and experimentation set by Gehry encouraged a whole series of architects in their forties and fifties – such as Thom Mayne, Michael Rotundi, Eric Owen

Right Peter Eisenman and Jaquelin Robertson, Wexner Center for the Visual Arts, The Ohio State University, Columbus, Ohio, 1983. In his first major public commission, Eisenman imposed the structural grids he had used to create earlier experimental houses on a tradtional campus plan. He inserted multi-gridded galleries between two bland modern theatres at a gentle angle and then anchored them with a complex fragment of a reconstructed armory – an ironic play on postmodern symbolism .

Moss, Craig Hodgetts, Robert Mangurian and the late Frank Israel – as well as younger talents such as Neil Denari. It also encouraged clients, who tend to be more adventurous in LA than their counterparts in other parts of the country. The work of these different architects was similar enough to be considered a school, but different enough not to be called a style. It was – and is – even more different from the new modernism emerging in New York, partly because Gehry's influence has led to a rather baroque form of expression, and partly because LA architects have many more opportunities to create freestanding buildings (most jobs in New York are for interiors within existing dwellings). Also, in LA, the architectural context is usually buildings that are low-rise and modern, rather than dense and historic. There are other differences, too: brighter colour is common in LA, as in most warm climates, and in this fantasy-filled city architects are more often inspired by popular culture than in the more hard-working, long-established and intellectual New York.

Although the context in which they work has less in common with Europe than does New York (which, as in European cities, is already built up), the architects of southern California have greater affinities with the European avant-garde that emerged in the 1980s and dominated the well-publicized MoMA exhibition, 'Deconstructivist Architecture', in 1988. Curated by Philip Johnson, this show was accompanied by a small exhibition of Russian Constructivist drawings from the museum's collection, giving it an air of both revivalism and radicalism. As an architect, Johnson had worked his way through the gamut of architectural languages: the International Style; a strange modern classicism (exemplified by the Lincoln Center); an angular version of modernism with triangles in plan and profile that Charles Jencks dubbed 'Late-Modernism' (Pennzoil Place); 'Post-Modern Classicism' (the AT&T Building); and other odd post-modern revivals (the Dutch Guildhall-revival Republic Bank). Now he was ready for something new. Of the featured architects only Bernard Tschumi actually used Constructivist forms, mostly at La Villette, although broken arcs, diagonals and interpenetrating planes did show up in the work of the other architects on show, namely Coop Himmelblau, Peter Eisenman, Frank Gehry, Zaha Hadid, Rem Koolhaas and Daniel Libeskind.

All the work in the exhibition was self-consciously and conspicuously modern, as well as symbolic. If there wasn't exactly applied decoration, there was certainly imagery. The work was almost the opposite of simple, cubic, plain-walled volumetric International Style modernism. Although it was really only Eisenman who invoked deconstructionist philosopher Jacques Derrida, the author of the catalogue essay, Mark Wigley, tried to link everything on view with deconstruction. Most reviewers

Right Frank Gehry, Guggenheim Museum, Bilbao, Spain, 1997. The baroque, almost fantastical, highly convoluted and amorphous forms of the Bilbao Guggenheim, built by Los Angeles' best-known architect, shout for attention. They represent the very antithesis of New York reductionism. Whereas in New York transparent, pared-down spaces are used to assimilate the new with historic buildings, the Guggenheim is ideal for a city, like Bilbao, requiring an architectural or cultural focus.

saw the show as an attempt at self-promotion, but with no other labels to hang on to, 'Decon' became the catch-phrase of the hour. It came to be used to describe a certain style of architecture using tilted planes, severed arcs and sharp metal edges. This style became increasingly common on the East Coast and can be seen in projects by younger New York architects such as Smith-Miller + Hawkinson, Hanrahan + Meyers, and Hariri + Hariri. This development can to a large extent be credited to Bernard Tschumi, who in the late 1980s replaced the post-modern contextualist James Stewart Polshek as Dean of the Graduate School of Architecture, Preservation and Planning at Columbia University. Tschumi exerts considerable influence through an increasingly varied body of built work and through his academic position, where he has encouraged aesthetic experimentation using computer technology.

The new modernism During the latter part of the 1990s, the frenetic energy of Decon has given way to something much quieter, more geometric and less decorous. It is often called 'minimalism' because of its sparse detail and at least superficial resemblance to the minimalist art of the 1960s and 70s. The connection is actually direct, since the most influential architect associated with the trend, Richard Gluckman, received his first commissions from patrons and dealers of the minimalists. Gluckman created the Dia Center for the Arts, a non-profit *kunsthalle* in a 3,700-square-metre (40,000-square-foot) warehouse in 1987. He did so largely by a process of subtraction. Old flooring, wall partitions and other incretions were removed to create bare concrete floors, walls and ceilings, using simple industrial lighting. Instead of a grand staircase, there are plain old fire stairs. The big, raw, open, high-ceilinged spaces are ideal, both in size and in character, for showing contemporary art. Gluckman went on to design galleries in SoHo for Mary Boone and Larry Gagosian, in the process introducing a new style of gallery design. Earlier, the norm had been open lofts on the upper floors of old cast-iron buildings, with long rows of classical columns painted white. Gluckman's were even larger, ground-floor spaces in single-storey structures with skylights and huge garage doors in front. Despite their industrial fittings and concrete floors, their simplicity, lighting, proportions and detailing made them seem almost Cistercian. Warehouse vernacular, in Gluckman's hands, created temples for art.

Gluckman subsequently graduated to designing museums. He renovated Marcel Breuer's Whitney Museum on Madison Avenue, a Brutalist gem that had once been marked for obliteration in a post-modern design by Michael Graves. He also created a larger version of the earlier garage gallery for Paula Cooper, with an elaborate wood truss ceiling. The gallery is situated near his pioneering Dia Center in west Chelsea, an area of New York where, when the center was built, empty warehouses stood near abandoned piers. Today, new gallery spaces are being created by other architects all around it in a similar style, and the Chelsea warehouse district is replacing SoHo as the centre of contemporary art. The raw simplicity of Chelsea is in tune with contemporary tastes, which are making themselves felt in some surprising places.

Bartholomew Voorsanger's crystalline marble, brass and bronze Garden Court at the Pierpont Morgan Library (1990) is about as far removed as can be from a concrete garage. The library, which displays antique manuscripts and drawings, was built in the Renaissance revival style by McKim, Mead & White in 1906, next door to the famous banker's house. (The house itself was replaced in 1928 by galleries that match the library.) Before Voorsanger was engaged, the institution had acquired a freestanding Italianate brownstone house behind the galleries, built in 1853, which had once belonged to Morgan's son. Compared with the 'correct' limestone library, the house was a more vertical (and typically American) version of the Renaissance revival style. One might have expected that the Garden Court would be designed to resemble the library, especially since a recent Renaissance revival addition to the Frick Museum had received an enthusiastic review from the *New York Times*' influential architecture critic, Paul Goldberger. Moreover, Voorsanger, although trained as a modernist, had been practising a simplified version of post-modernism in the 1970s and 80s (with Edward Mills, who later returned to modernism on his own). The fact that the house was faced in a different material from the library, and had very different proportions, made any connection strategy complicated. Voorsanger's decision to join the two with a Corbusian modern addition in rich veined white marble and limestone, oxidized brass and bronze, seeded art glass and transparent panes, all crowned by a great piano curve roof, was surprising. The acquiescence of the conservative trustees was even more so.

Instead of replicating the old, the new garden court was related to the original buildings by contrast, as earlier modern additions to historic buildings had tried to do (and as modernist theory and most preservation guidelines required). It did so much more successfully than most earlier attempts, partly because it was as sumptuous as the original and partly because it responded to the older buildings with understanding, respect and confidence — as an equal partner. Despite its considerable cost ($12 million), the addition has turned out to be an economic boon as it generates $600,000 a year in revenue from party rentals, a fact that was not overlooked by the Asia Society when it hired Voorsanger this year to create a similar courtyard at its Park Avenue galleries, designed by Edward

Larrabee Barnes in 1981. The Morgan court successfully proved that modernism could provide the same elegance and delight that historic architecture had – or could do so even better.

Although born-again classicists still have plenty of work, many architects who experimented with post-modern classicism are now returning to modernism. Even the big firms are jumping on the bandwagon: Skidmore, Owings & Merrill, which built new versions of Art Deco in the 1980s, hired minimalist Frank Lupo in 1997. The chief designer at Kohn Pedersen Fox, William Pedersen, has revived the modern vocabulary of his early buildings and is now designing some of the strongest buildings of his career. James Stewart Polshek, who has blended old and new fabric artfully, knowledgably and with good sense, today uses mostly modern forms. Alexander Gorlin, a younger architect, critic and historian with a small firm, who worked with equal finesse in modern and classical idioms (and built the first modern house in the New Urbanist enclave of Seaside, Florida) is bringing the same wit and irony to modern designs that he worked into historicizing antecedents. While good modern architects such as Bruce Graham and Edward Larrabee Barnes seemed to produce weaker work when they adopted post-modernism, the reverse appears to be true when the best talents return to modernism after a historicizing fling.

Modern architecture is even inching into the mainstream of US society. But this is not by building the sanitary flats and humane factories that the early European modernists envisioned, but via clothing stores and consumer products. (This is America, after all.) About a mile north of the Morgan Library on Madison Avenue, between 60th and 72nd streets, a series of boutiques tells the story of style in the last decade. On the northern edge, Ralph Lauren purchased a turn-of-the-century 'chateau' that had been converted to apartments and shops and, with interior designer Naomi Leff, turned it back into a house – or at least a store that looked like one – in 1988. Sweaters are stored in bedroom drawers; suits hang in dressing-room closets; antique furniture, oil paintings and oriental rugs foster the same illusion of aristocratic elegance as the designer does in his clothes.

A few blocks south, at 60th Street, Calvin Klein built its opposite number in 1996: a minimalist boutique designed by John Pawson. It is as in keeping with his plain, structured, modern clothes as Lauren's historically reminiscent mansion is with his revivalist 'polo' gear. In between, new shops for well-known designers by different architects open every few months. Michael Gabellini, who designs the Jil Sander stores everywhere, did one for Searle. Sadly, a tiny boutique and a store for the Pace Furniture company, both designed by Steven Holl in the late 1980s, have been replaced. Holl,

Above Frank Gehry, Gehry House, Santa Monica, California, 1978. The rear view of Gehry's Californian pink bungalow which he sabotaged by eschewing elements, such as windows, and inserting new features in unhomey materials, such as corrugated iron and chain link.

like Gluckman and the husband-wife team of Tod Williams and Billie Tsien, is an important influence on younger architects who are now doing spare modern stores of their own. David Piscuskas of 1100 Architect, who created the Metro Pictures gallery in Chelsea, designs the J Crew stores in New York. Deborah Berke has designed stores for CK (Calvin Klein Jeans) and Club Monaco. She also created the bare concrete and steel offices of Baron & Baron, the advertising and package design firm responsible for Calvin Klein's minimalist perfume bottles.

All in all, it seems, little has changed since the 1930s – modern architecture still serves art and fashion more than it serves social needs. But there is one important exception. The current Director of Architecture for the New York City Housing Authority, David Burney, has been inviting many of the city's best talents to design new community centres at housing projects. The idea is to redirect youthful energy into sports and, at the same time, fill barren plazas in 'tower in the park' landscapes. One of the most original is a scheme by Wayne Berg of Pasanella + Klein Stolzman + Berg for the Williamsburg Houses in Brooklyn. This is the only *seidlung*-style housing project in New York, and was designed by William Lescaze and a group of architects in 1939. The Williamsburg centre will be built at the end of an asphalt 'park' with basketball courts, playing fields and a playground surrounded by a chain-link fence. Where others saw urban alienation, Berg saw defensible space and a secure environment where players could watch and be watched – as well as a material that Frank Gehry had made architectural by using it on his own house (the Williamsburg Community Center is to be made of chain link and other industrial materials). Berg's sensitive treatment of the materials and the space is giving the area the same kind of raw beauty that Gluckman brought to warehouses for viewing art.

During all the years that post-modern classicism flourished and much serious architecture was put to frivolous purposes, one New York architect kept the dream of the early modern pioneers alive. Michael Sorkin spent the first half of his career mainly as a critic for the alternative newspaper, *The Village Voice*, championing out-of-fashion architects such as Marcel Breuer and Paul Rudolph and calling attention to the antics of powerful figures like Philip Johnson and Paul Goldberger. With passion, wit, moral courage, a discerning eye, sharp tongue and big heart, he has argued the case for modernism in the fullest, most idealistic sense of the word. He still writes much more than he builds, but his utopian urban designs are now attracting attention even in established circles. Modern architecture in the US may still be mainly in the service of an aesthetic elite, but architects like Sorkin are waiting in the wings, ready to effect a takeover if ever they get the chance.

1 The word 'post-modern', with a hyphen, is here used as it was in the 1970s and 1980s to denote a specific kind of historically-reminiscent architecture that appeared as a reaction to the International Style. It should not be confused with the broader sense in which the word 'postmodern' is usually used today, without a hyphen, to mean the attitude, derived from postmodern philosophy, that rejects the notion of progress and accepts the priniciple of uncertainty. To avoid confusion, I shall avoid the use of that term.

2 It was actually Johnson who organized the Salon des Refusés, in 1931, with Alfred Barr and the art dealer Julian Levy, in a storefront on 57th Street near the Museum of Modern Art's temporary headquarters, for the International Style architects who had not been invited to participate in the prestigious annual exhibition at the Architectural League. Unsatisfied with its critical reception in the press, he even wrote a review of it for *Creative Arts* (June 1931, pp433–5). Johnson later became the museum's first curator of architecture and design, went on to design its first two additions, and continues to play an active role in MoMA affairs to this day. He donated his important art collection to the institution in 1997.

3 The book emphasized the work of Le Corbusier, Mies and Gropius but also included the work of numerous German, Scandinavian, Russian, Swiss and other European architects and a few Americans who toed the party line. 'Aalto, not Wright is illustrated in the book, since he had already shifted from Swedish Neoclassicism to the International Style in the 1920s,' Hitchcock explained. And the book emphasized not its social objectives but its physical properties, which the authors identified as: 'Architecture as Volume, Surfacing Material [which was supposed to emphasize the continuity of the wall plane and not suggest mass], Regularity [which reflected the structural system and suggested the use of standard parts], and the Avoidance of Applied Ornament,' (quoted from Hitchcock's foreword to the 1966 paperback edition, pix).

4 This provision in the US zoning code allows developers to build more floors that would normally be allowable so long as they commit to specified extras, such as adding a public plaza, incorporating a theatre, or preserving a landmarked building.

5 New York City represents something of an exception to this generalization, since no stigma is attached to high-rise housing (because all classes live in it). Also, since housing in New York is unusually expensive, a broader spectrum of society lives in publicly subsidized housing. Most of the projects actually function quite well. No towers have been demolished, and the New York City Housing Authority houses most of its 500,000 tenants successfully. Still, most people prefer low-rise blocks, and the high-rise apartments built for the private sector are on traditional streets, not set off in Voisin 'parks' like public housing used to be. Even the new public housing is low-rise and integrated.

6 Later he founded another at the University of Pennsylvania which had a simlar impact in Philadelphia, although that city had always been more historically aware and less brutally commercial than New York.

7 He founded and directed the Institute for Architecture and Urban Studies, an independent think-tank which between 1967 and 1983 brought architects to New York from all over the world to show and talk about their work.

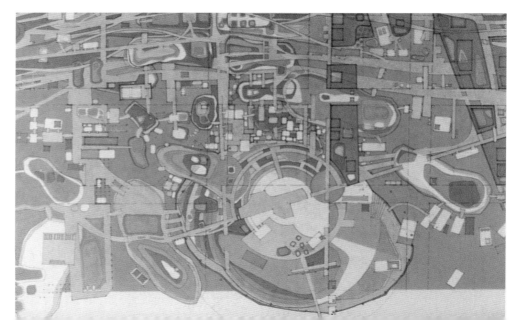

Right Michael Sorkin, Master Plan for Brooklyn Waterfront, New York, 1993–4. Despite the emphasis on the physical quality of space, which is now so pervasive in New York architecture, a few designers have continued to insist on a brand of modernism that has a wider application for society as a whole. This project for a mixed-use recreational environment was undertaken as a counterproposal to official planning for a stretch of disused piers. Park components – gardens, tennis courts and restaurants – were to be created out of barges refitted on site.

We believe that the tenants of modernism, first learned from the late 1960s and early 1970s second-generation modernists at university, and as manifest by our exposure to minimalist artists in the mid-1970s, have been a consistent and continually evolving aspect of our practice, whether it is applied to renovation work or new work. Richard Gluckman.[1]

The conversion of a vacant 3,700-square-metre (40,000-square-foot) four-storey industrial building, in a desolate part of Manhattan, into an exhibition space for a non-profit avant-garde art foundation, took place as the post-modern movement in architecture was running out of steam. Instead of capitalizing on the building's quaint old features (which in any case were few and far between), as earlier gallery conversions in SoHo had done, Richard Gluckman emphasized the raw industrial quality of the concrete structure – its space, barrenness, strength and unfinished materials.

He did this by removing partitions, flooring, wallboard and false ceilings. The new bare concrete floors, plain painted walls and exposed conduit, combined with the industrial grey and white colour scheme, share the aesthetic of the works of art they contain, rather than provide contrast in the way that most wood-floored, colonnaded, human-scaled galleries of the time

did. Like a minimalist sculptor, Gluckman works with the rudiments of his medium, in this case proportion and lighting.

This approach was to change the prevailing style of gallery design and even set the tone for fancy shops and loft apartments. But here it was developed in response to a specific brief. The primary purpose of the gallery was the extended display of large-scale artworks. The brief stipulated that exhibitions were to be shown for up to a year, before a new artist's work was installed. As Gluckman's office points out: 'The challenge inherent in this project was to create an appropriate context for the art on display without compromising the basic, strongly articulated structural language of the building. The electrical grid had to be flexible for changing installations but also had to demonstrate a permanent sense of detail.'[2]

The details and finishes were pared down to ensure that the exhibited works were not overwhelmed by the architecture. As visitors work their way up the building, the structural features become less apparent and space and light – the media through which art is displayed – become more and more predominant. The skeleton of the structure, most evident on the second floor, is absorbed on the third floor and almost disappears by the fourth floor.

Richard Gluckman
Dia Art Foundation
New York, 1987

1 Written in response to some questions put to the architect by Helen Castle in April 1998.
2 From the project description supplied by Richard Gluckman's office in April 1998.

Opposite Exterior of the Dia Art
Foundation, marked out by its portico
and a Joseph Beuys installation, which
consists of a tree and a 2-metre piece
of basalt. **Above left** The gallery space
on the second floor, where the beams
and structure of the building are at their
most apparent. **Above right** The
gallery on the third floor, where the
ceiling's skeleton is less prominent.
Right Light becomes the main medium
for modelling space on the top floor of
the gallery. The large windows also give
the upper floor impressive views of the
New York skyline.

The success of the Dia Art Foundation not only led to a revolution in gallery design in New York but also reinvigorated the surrounding area – an area which in the 1980s was full of abandoned workshops and factories, used for storage, and where the sidewalks were empty. Today the West Chelsea area is lined with commercial art galleries, while restaurants are opening and highly desirable lofts – in the minimalist style of course – are being carved out of warehouse floors. Even many of the veteran SoHo galleries, such as Paula Cooper's, are moving in. This renovation of a 460-square-metre (5,000-square-foot) warehouse for Cooper is a quintessential example of the 'garage style', which Gluckman invented in SoHo where he created galleries for Mary Boone and Larry Gagosian in less ideal spaces.

The original building for the Paula Cooper Gallery had a dramatic double-height interior, with a bare wood truss-roof structure and brick walls. By adding new steel trusses Gluckman was able to remove the columns from the main gallery area, thus providing a clear span and a soaring well of space. To provide natural illumination and reinforce the proportions of the room Gluckman inserted skylights above the joists, without disrupting the line of the roof. He also incorporated artificial lighting into the roof structure. Although the heating ducts have been exposed, as in the Dia Art Foundation, they have been located where their impact is minimal.

Three new elements have been introduced – a freight lift, a stairway and a mezzanine – in a way which enhances existing features. The stairs and the lift frame the entrance to the main gallery space. The 120-square-metre (1,300-square-foot) mezzanine, which houses offices, a private showroom and a library, overlooks the main gallery and contains the entrance on the ground floor.

Many original brick walls remain exposed, as do the wood rafters which have been cleaned and lightly whitewashed to increase their reflective qualities. Although painted gypsum wallboard and a reinforced tinted, terrazzo-ground concrete floor have been installed, the essential character of the raw industrial space remains. The building's original facade has even been preserved; this has been done by realigning the masonry openings and by using steel window frames and doors. The steel frames are carried through into the interior, where they are used around openings.

Richard Gluckman
Paula Cooper Gallery
New York, 1996

Opposite above Situated above the street-level entrance is the mezzanine, accommodating administration offices, with a window looking over the large gallery space. **Opposite below** The preserved facade of the Paula Cooper Gallery with new steel window and door frames. **Above** The raw quality of the building and its industrial scale makes it ideal for displaying large contemporary works of art. **Left** Here the effectiveness of lighting the gallery from skylights and with spotlights attached to the roof joists is apparent.

About 1.5 kilometres (1 mile) due north of the Dia Art Foundation, in a thriving but dull industrial area on the western edge of the garment district, a fourteen-storey industrial building with enormous windows houses the offices of architects Vignelli Associates; Gwathmey Siegel; Buttrick, White & Burtis (the successor firm to McKim, Mead & White); and Richard Meier. Architects' offices all over New York are housed in similar quarters, but Meier's stand out from the crowd, distinguished by their absolute rigour of conception and their careful modulation of light and space.

Unlike the other office spaces in the same building, which are cut off from the elevator bank by solid walls or opened to it completely by tall glass doors, Meier's are approached by a fully enclosed low-ceilinged lobby. The white perpendicular walls are partly filled with grids of glass bricks. Light enters from the spaces beyond but no views of the inner sanctum are offered. The entry leads to a long, narrow space, all white, with a plain white desk on the left facing the centre and three large all-white architectural models on pedestals under plexiglas lined up on the right . A half-height wall behind them, left absolutely bare, admits light from the enormous, high-ceilinged work area behind it. Here, light floods in from gargantuan south-facing windows, which reflects off all-white

work tables, partitions and ceilings. Long, wide, extremely orderly rows of worktables – divided occasionally by partial walls that extend the entire length or width of the space – create regular subdivisions, but the sense of one gigantic white space overrides the divisions. The homely adage, 'a place for everything and everything in its place', has meaning here as nowhere else. Clutter is inconceivable – even a pile of papers out of place is hard to imagine. Book shelves and cabinets contain all loose materials. Rectangular racks next to desks hold rolled-up drawings. The 90-degree angle rules, on both a macro and a micro scale.

Richard Meier can hardly be termed a minimalist. His recent work (such as the City Hall in The Hague or the Contemporary Art Museum in Barcelona) has burst out of the early Corbusian mode, and expressive curves and complex spatial interpenetrations are constantly at play, while volumes are becoming weighty. But his own workspace possesses the discipline, the almost spiritual quality of light and the reductive rigour associated with minimalism – and typical of modernism in New York today. And the palette it uses is predominantly monochromatic, with sharp black and white contrasts. Geometry governs every move, and less is most certainly more, as it is in everything we call minimalist.

Richard Meier
Offices of Richard Meier
& Partners
New York, 1986

Above The spareness of reductionism, with its emphasis on the concealment of the extraneous, makes it ideal for environments which require a high degree of rationalization – such as disciplined work situations. This approach has been successfully applied in the rigorous organization of Meier's office, where architects have been provided with large work surfaces and adequate storage space for files and drawings. The grid-like layout of the white work tables reflects the austerity of the existing horizontal and vertical structural elements.

The Williamsburg Community Center is inspired by the chain-link fences that surround the existing asphalt-paved park, and define the ball courts and playgrounds within, rather than by the architecture of the housing project it is being constructed to serve. The centre is one of dozens that are currently being designed by talented New York architects for the New York City Housing Authority. Most of the new centres are intended to fill barren plazas in postwar 'tower in the park'-style housing schemes; and are designed to provide a place for young people to come to, so that they stay out of trouble. The context of this centre, however, is very different.

The Williamsburg Houses are long, low-rise International Style blocks, arranged in rows which are diagonal to the street grid. The site for the community centre is at the end of a park, where there are few trees and a large number of playing fields. The architect, Wayne Berg, realized that the playing fields are popular and safe because the chain-link fencing, which surrounds them, makes them visible from the street. Perhaps conditioned by Frank Gehry's use of the material in his own house (see page 76), he saw beauty in the open metal fencing.

The Williamsburg Community Center is designed to convey a sense of openness and enclosure at the same time. The walls are composed of a series of garage and aircraft hangar doors, made from heat-strenthened glass. These can be opened so as to combine interior and exterior space, acting in the same way as does the security fence surrounding the adjacent playground. Transparent, flexible interior walls also provide views from one activity area to another, and make it possible to partition off unused spaces.

**Pasanella + Klein
Stolzman + Berg**
Wiliamsburg Community
Center, New York
due for completion 2000

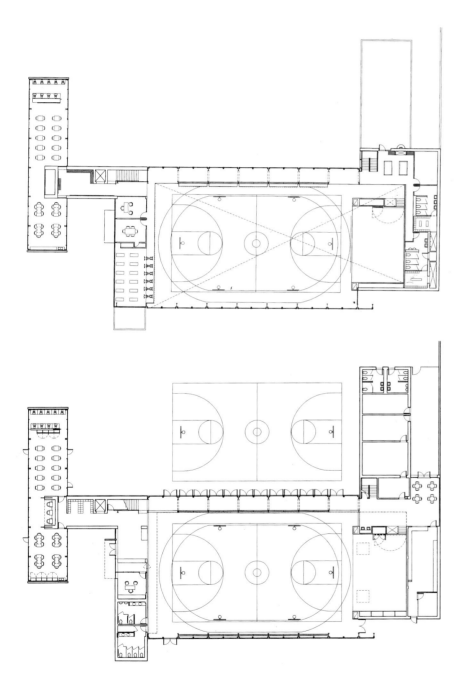

Opposite Computer renderings of the interior of the Williamsburg Community Center, where street-tough industrial materials will create adaptable interior recreational spaces with the openness and character of an urban playground in a refined but direct way. **Left** First and ground-floor plans of the flexible centre, showing how spaces can accommodate athletic activities. **Above** The model of the exterior of the centre shows how it will be possible to see into and through the big, open rectangular spaces the way you can see into and through the playing fields next door.

It is essential for architecture to use light to articulate space. One must think how to use natural light in many different ways. I employ only very basic geometric forms and then the light makes everything very interesting.
Yoshio Taniguchi.[1]

When MoMA (the Museum of Modern Art) decided to expand its facilities – for the fifth time in fifty years – it began the selection and programming process with a series of lectures designed to enable its trustees to proceed as knowledgably as possible. The series was unusual for its relative openness – both to ideas and to the general public – and for the way it looked backwards as well as forwards. After all, modernism in the past broke sharply with tradition and looked to the future only.

The first lecture, by MoMA's new director, Glenn Lowry, recounted the history of the museum's building programme. This began in 1939, when Philip L Goodwin and Edwin Durrell Stone built the museum's first permanent home, the planar white marble International Style building on West 53rd Street. Philip Johnson added a black Miesian wing on the west side in 1951, built the Abby Aldrich Rockefeller Sculpture Garden (behind the original museum) two years later and in 1964

added the almost neoclassical, arcaded East Wing. Designing the West Wing in 1983, Cesar Pelli opened the interior with escalators, extended the museum into the former Whitney Museum building on West 54th Street, reconfigured the gallery layout, and erected a luxury apartment tower on the southwest corner, which was intended to support the museum financially. Little more than a decade later, however, the museum decided it needed still more space (and money) and acquired two townhouses, together with the Dorset Hotel, situated behind the tower on 54th Street. Plans for the addition (which will double the size of the facilities), and the search for an architect, began in 1996. This involved meetings, retreats and a tour by the architecture committee of architects' offices and buildings which took them to thirty-one countries.

In the US at least, Yoshio Taniguchi was the least well known of the ten semi-finalists (see page 64) who in spring 1997 were invited to submit sketchbooks of ideas. His contribution, however, was one of the most straightforward, clear and rational. The three semi-finalists who were shortlisted – Jacques Herzog and Pierre de Meuron, and Bernard Tschumi, as well as Taniguchi – had all presented quiet, articulate and complete sets of sketches. They all demonstrated that they had thought through the

Yoshio Taniguchi
Expansion and renovation of
the Museum of Modern Art
New York
design proposal 1997–8

Left Model showing aerial view from the northeast of the Abby Aldrich Rockefeller Sculpture Garden.
Opposite Model showing MoMA's West 53rd Steet facade, incorporating the white marble elevation of Goodwin and Durrell Stone's original International Style building of 1939 and Philip Johnson's black Miesan wing of 1951. On the southwest corner is Cesar Pelli's 1983 apartment tower.

problem thoroughly, and that they were trying to solve the puzzle of the expansion without upstaging or undermining the existing fabric. In the final round, the other two contenders added more expressive elements but Taniguchi continued on the path that had led to his initial selection. His design of plain, white-walled, rectangular galleries resembles those of MoMA's earlier wings, as well as those in his own museums in Japan, which are shaped and enlivened by light.

Taniguchi's scheme is distinguished by the way it integrates the new parts of the building with the existing and renovated fabric, enhancing them in measured, subtle ways. The circulation system for the museum has been rethought so that the Abby Aldrich Rockefeller Sculpture Garden, the museum's best-loved feature, is given a central position and expanded to its pre-1983 size. The main entrance is to be moved from 53rd to 54th Street. Visitors will enter a light-filled passageway between the two streets and immediately encounter the garden lengthways, without obstruction, rather than entering the garden in the middle as they do now (which allows only a shallow view through the escalators).

The scheme also involved renovation of the existing building. The Goodwin and Stone facade on 53rd Street is to regain its original piano-shaped canopy and become the entrance to a newly expanded film and video centre; the 'Bauhaus staircase' is to be restored and become a prominent connection between departmental galleries; and the base of the Pelli apartment tower will be revealed from inside the museum for the first time.

Essential to the overall architectural conception is Taniguchi's insistence on the importance of scale. He explains: 'I am always trying to visualize my spaces relative to scale. But it is not just the works that are important, the space has to be relative to human scale. So, therefore, when I am working with models in my office, I am always putting the scale figures in them. I always return to the human scale.'[2] The three main levels of the new western galleries have varying ceiling heights, with generous floor areas and wall surfaces, enabling even the largest art works to be displayed.

It is Taniguchi's use of light as an architectural medium, however, that best displays his understanding of museum and exhibition-space design. By including graduated set-backs with glass inserts along their roof lines and numerous skylights in his galleries, he maximizes the amount of diffused natural light that is introduced. It is this natural light that brings the museum's objects to life.

1 'Interview with Yoshio Taniguchi', *MoMA: The Magazine of the Museum of Modern Art*, March 1998, p5.
2 Ibid.

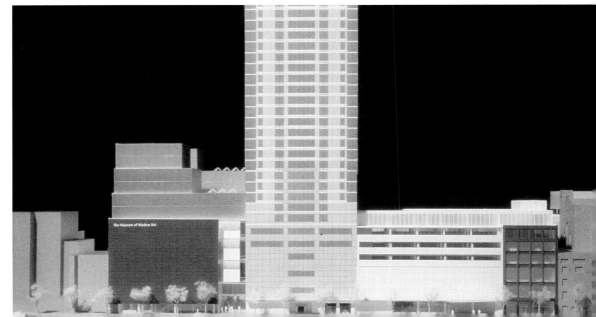

Even modernist architects not usually associated with a minimalist approach have been known to work in a manner that shares the discipline, reductiveness and understatement typical of New York modernism of the late 1980s and 1990s. When it came to designing his own Chelsea loft, Bernard Tschumi (who has been variously associated with neo-constructivism, deconstructivism, and a unique kind of high-tech expressionism) eliminated more than he added. His additions, moreover, are ordered with the rigour of the best minimalist art.

The 17th Street loft is situated about 1.5 kilometres (1 mile) southeast of the Dia Art Foundation in a thriving neighbourhood where Art Deco apartment buildings, publishing houses and high-end retail stores coexist. The original space measured 40 metres (130 feet) by 9 metres (30 feet), with concrete ceiling beams spanning its width. A colonnade ran the length of the space on one side, with fourteen large windows running down the other (south) side. Tschumi left the central area open for an enormous living and dining room. He covered the floors with ebony-stained oak, except in the bathrooms where he used black ceramic tile, and painted all the walls, beams and columns white. A freestanding box running almost the full length of the space contains bedrooms, bathrooms and a kitchen. Behind it, on the long

north wall, there is a corridor and art wall with a narrow shelf for architectural models. A black metal floor-to-ceiling bookcase, with space on each side, marks the end of the main living area. Workspace is partitioned off at each end. Light fixtures are attached to pipes along the window wall and to the sides of the bedroom-box.

The main living space is completely empty apart from a few original early modern tubular steel-and-black leather chairs, and a black dining-room table. The only colour comes from books, flowers and works of art. Even functional elements, such as the evenly spaced pipes, radiators, pilasters and columns, which are all painted white, contribute to the rigour of the overall scheme.

First used by the architect to live and work in himself, the loft is now exclusively a family apartment. The architect's professional office now occupies a floor of its own in the same building. Another study in black and white, it is ordered with the same almost obsessive discipline.

Bernard Tschumi
Residential loft
New York, 1988

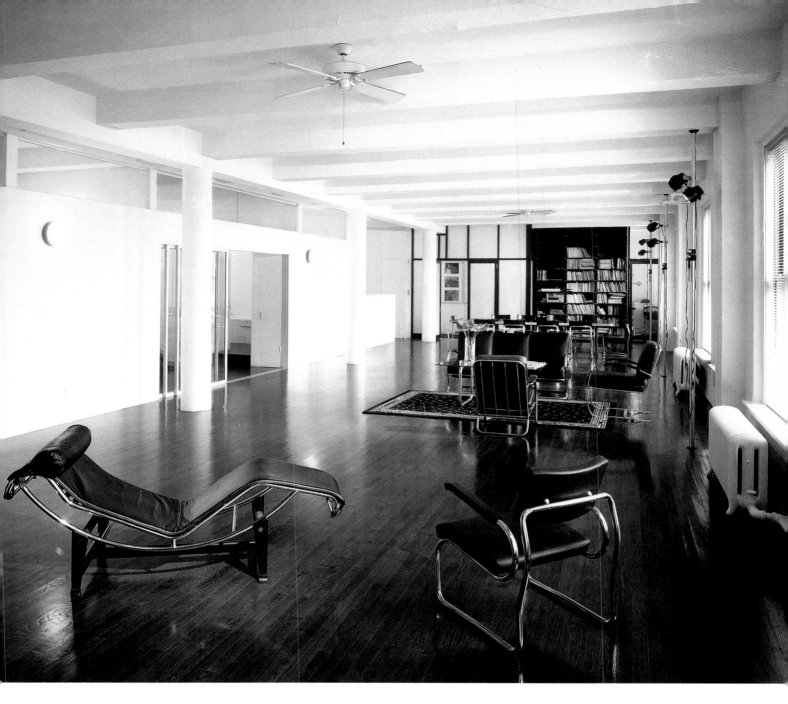

Opposite above The original colonnade, running along one side of the main living-room area, echoes the vertical supports of the wall of windows on the south side. **Opposite below** A corridor lines the north wall of the apartment, providing space for hanging drawings and a shelf for models on one side, and defining private spaces on the other. **Above and right** Views of the living–dining–work area from either end of the room. The original, early modern leather-and-steel tubular furniture reinforces the structural elements and provides a sense of history, while the ebony-stained oak floor injects a contemporary richness.

The project layers a palimpsestic reading of public space, analogical to a city that never was but could and perhaps should have been. The space excels in such subtle allusions and delicate critical remarks. The building suggests without imposing.
Livio Dimitriu.[1]

The Pierpont Morgan Library's three main buildings have long been separated by a garden, which over the years has been encroached upon and reduced in size. We chose to reconnect the tripartite ensemble not through the garden's elimination but through its irrevocable presence in a new spatial dynamic.

The design of the court evolved intentionally, rationally and specifically to solve many practical problems. On an aesthetic level we wished to respect its adjacent neighbours not by mimicking them, but by establishing an independence. We chose to do this by designing a glazed court, which connects the earlier buildings to each other and has a dialectical relationship with them. The older buildings provide an intense interior experience with their dark woods, marbles and mosaics of extraordinary quality. For the connecting court we wanted to give an equally intense exterior experience, expressed through materiality, space, sequence and movement.

The court's glazed profile evolved to meet particular requirements that arose. Firstly, it was shaped to provide enough light to grow the small, black olive trees, proposed by the landscape architect Dan Kiley. An important consideration was the unknown structural capacity of the adjacent buildings, which meant we could not risk bearing any significant additional weight on their walls. This manifested

in the built court in a solution that structurally transferred the weight of the skylight to a 165-metre (540-foot) transverse longitudinal beam. The perimeter elevation of the skylight was designed to start and end at the north and south elevations so as not to favour any one building. The height of the skylight and its double-breaking curve towards the south also had to be profiled to eliminate its visible presence while standing at the 36th Street entrance to the main library. In addition, the Madison Avenue west elevation was set back to make it less apparent from the corner of 36th and Madison.

One of the later design additions was the one-storey Madison Avenue projection, which enabled the court to mediate between the scale of the existing building and the street. Lastly, a mechanical cooling and heating solution was developed. This has proved an ingenious means of conserving energy: air is stratified horizontally within the court, but only the lower 5 metres (15 feet) of air are cooled and heated; the upper air remains untreated.

Though the Garden Court emerged as a completely unexpected part of the master plan to expand the Pierpont Morgan Library, its passage through planning was nevertheless anticipated to be a difficult one – given that a modern design was to be juxtaposed with the well-known and revered original library. Any

Bart Voorsanger
Garden Court
Pierpont Morgan Library
New York, 1990

*Project description
by the architect*

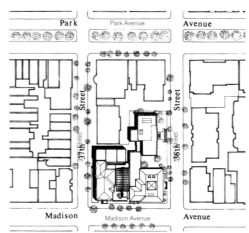

exterior modification of the existing buildings required the approval of the New York City Landmark Preservation Commission.

While our design was in progress, the Commission established an important precedent – albeit after much debate – by approving Kevin Roche's seamless new addition to the 5th Avenue mansion, which houses the Jewish Museum, in a historicizing style. Nevertheless, I felt our strategy had to be different; I believe we have to have confidence in contemporary design as a visual language which is capable of expressing energy and cultural ambition, even within a historic context. For the court to succeed, I felt it needed to rise to the level of spirit and material evident in the original McKim, Mead & White library. Architecturally, we wanted the court to be a place of mediation and meditation. It had to be original both spatially and in its quality of light, with materials, trees and flowering plants acting as counterparts to the original.

The resulting design offers something quite new, with its sense of exterior light filtering through the trees and skylight. Reflections are created by the metallic pewter surfaces, while the light marble floors add a visual fluidity. The court's relatively small size belies its impact. It shows how the positive, radical transformation of a fragment of architecture can make a real contribution to an existing institution.

1 CE Pierce, L Dimitriu and B Voorsanger, *The Pierpont Morgan Library: Garden Court and Master Plan Expansion*, USA Books (New York), 1996, p14.

Opposite above View of the upper level, which provides access to the library annexe in the neighbouring brownstone via a lift. **Opposite below** Site plan showing the Garden Court's location on Madison Avenue. It is built on the site of the brownstone's garden, to its left, which is now an annexe of the original library, to the court's right. **Above** Interior of the Garden Court; the planting of olive trees alludes to the original garden on which it is sited.

The wonder of the Modern Movement
lay in the search for something new, and this still applies today.
During the 1980s, much of the vacuity of modern architecture at its worst was challenged,
an experience which was to some extent cathartic.
At the lowest level, it resulted in a post-modern architecture
that was no more than nostalgia, drawing freely on historical references –
a sad dismissal of a more rooted investigation. It did, however,
bring to modern architecture an unarticulated need for something more than a clean platonic minimalism – namely, a new awareness of site, place and environment.

My search along these lines started at college. We tended to be force-fed a
modernist party line: Le Corbusier, Mies van der Rohe, Walter Gropius and Alvar Aalto, though
not enough of the latter. This was tinged with moralistic overtones. There was a great emphasis
on truth of materials and the need to express structure. What, however, impressed me when I
experienced works of the modern masters for myself – Ronchamp, La Tourette, IIT – was the
content, the spirit of the work, which operates outside its rhetoric. This essence was enforced
with a vengeance when I encountered the work of Frank Lloyd Wright and Louis Kahn, in particular, with whom architecture had its beginnings in the poetic. While working for Charles Adams
in Fort Worth, in the tradition of Wright, I began to understand Wright's relentless organic
thought processes. Most importantly, there exists in his buildings a site-specificity that has a
consistency of intention. Although it can be found in Wright's designs throughout the United States –
Taliesin East is just as rooted in the landscape as is Taliesin West – it is most apparent in his
work in the West.

In the US there is a kind of theoretical 'continental divide'. The East has strong
European leanings, with a tradition of eclectic architecture. Its attitudes towards 'real estate', as
against the land, as well as its cultural axis, have tended to look towards Europe. On the East Coast,
the survey grid was originally built on a Jeffersonian model, which treated land as a commodity rather
than a cherished resource. Although land was similarly treated in the West and the Southwest, where
it was divided up by the Spanish monarchy and the Roman Catholic Church, the imposition of the grid
was far less pervasive. In New Mexico and Mexico, meanwhile, the surviving structures of pre-
Columbian civilizations were so breathtaking that they could not be completely obliterated, even

Empathy versus Ideas   *Antoine Predock*

A Personal Account

of American Modernism

in the West

though Spanish missions attempted, in some cases, to build over these sacred places. The highly sensitive positioning of these ancient Anasazi sites took into account shelter and vantage points, and was shaped by cosmology.

The boundary between the two sides of the continent is not simply geographical. The Eurocentric bias is a benign virus that has spread from east to west. Whereas in the early days it resulted in a European eclecticism, it now manifests itself in the adoption of European theoretical models by certain West Coast schools and practices. This intellectual inclination at times ignores its own orientation and its location on the Pacific Ocean that has been so inspiring for all those cultures whose shores its waters touch.

Nevertheless, there are important contemporary architects in the West who have made site-specificity the focus of their work. Back in the 1960s and 70s, Judith Chaffee was designing houses that were attuned to site and climatic response. Today, Michael Rotundi is taking a much deeper look at site. Another architect who has worked in the desert a long time is Will Bruder. There is always a strong element of site-specificity in his work, and he is a master at paring down materials to their essentials. Other younger architects include Wendell Burnette, who although largely self-educated, trained for three years at Taliesin West and worked for over a decade in Bruder's office.

This architecture poses a real alternative to the continuing erasure of Native American precedents. When travelling east to west, this erasure is made evident to any architect by the Western 'ghost towns' with their *ersatz* classical buildings. Their appliquéd ornament and wooden classical pediments were used as a security blanket against the great, daunting landscape. When the first settlers came, instead of looking to the buildings of the native peoples they tried to replace them with something familiar from another place. They wanted something cosy and European, as respite from the great expanse that surrounded them.

What cries out to be explored, however, is the very thing that this continuing habit turns its back on: the vast landscape, with its ineffable space. The landscape needs to be read physically and metaphysically in order to draw on its sacred power. Great architecture – whether it is at Chaco Canyon, Chartres, Salisbury or Kyoto, or whether it is certain works of the modern masters which I first encountered at college – depends on this reading of landscape, in terms of the physical, the cultural and the spiritual.

Antoine Predock's conceptual sketches of his buildings demonstrate the extent to which he visualizes architecture in terms of its setting. The line between the built and natural environment often becomes blurred. Sometimes the landscape predominates, as in his sketch for the Spencer Theater, where the theatre appears as a rocky outcrop. **Previous page** CLA Building, CAL Poly, Pomona, California, 1992. **Right** Nelson Fine Arts Center, Tempe, Arizona, 1989. **Opposite above** Turtle Creek House, Dallas, Texas, 1993. **Opposite below** Spencer Theater for Performing Arts, Alto, New Mexico, 1997.

Built for keen birdwatchers, this house is finely tuned to the surrounding avifauna as well as its natural setting. The location was chosen as a vantage point for bird observation. Its site is on major north–south migratory flight paths, where eastern and western bird habitats converge. Positioned along a prehistoric trail, it follows the Austin limestone formation in a landscape where woodlands, prairie and stream overlap. To allude to this geological presence and ancient memories, limestone ledges form the house's foreground. By containing local plant life, these ledges also encourage birds to occupy the area. The entrance foyer, or fissure, of the house creates a central point of departure for access to the various observation points, and to the north and south wings. The south wing is designed for formal social gatherings and private retreat, while the north wing is devoted to the informal and the everyday. A third zone, the roofscape, creates the focus of the house. Walkways over the house allow the occupants to survey birds, and any arriving guests. An intimate rooftop arena, closer to the parapet, is inwardly focused while also providing a shielded cover for outward viewing. The central steel 'sky ramp' projects the entrance fissure into the canopy of trees and beyond to the sky.

A highly sophisticated house, designed for entertaining as well as for ordinary domestic use, Turtle Creek is able to reach out to nature and its site's ancient past while accommodating its occupants' modern needs in a wholly contemporary style.

Antoine Predock
Turtle Creek House
Dallas, Texas, 1993

Opposite above View of the house showing the south wing, for formal events, to the left, and the north wing, which houses the private living areas, to the right. **Opposite below** Limestone ledges in front of the house create an attractive habitat for local birds. **Above** The main room in the south wing. **Right** The entrance fissure, or foyer, that conjoins the north and south wings and the sky ramps for birdwatching. This formal entrance allows visitors to have access to the ramps on social occasions without intruding on the private living areas of the house.

The Spencer Theater represents the culmination of the client and architect's search for a convergence between the theatre of landscape and the theatre of performance. Located in the middle of Fort Stanton Mesa in southern New Mexico, it is situated along the axis of the summer sun and is positioned half-way between Sunset Peak on the east horizon and Sierra Blanca to the west. It is Sierra Blanca, the white mountain, which provides the initial locus for the building's form and position. A sculpted limestone mass, the theatre has been excavated to accommodate finely balanced relationships between light, views, performance and procession. Designed to be used all year around, the theatre is occupied by various touring companies.

Antoine Predock
Spencer Theater for the
Performing Arts
Alto, New Mexico, 1997

The wedge-like form of the theatre is presented as a sculpted, monolithic piece of stone that has forced its way up from beneath the fragile crust of the *mesa*. Lodged within a fissure and erupting from the north flank, it features a crystalline, chandelier-like shell of laminated glass which links the vertical procession to the upper lobby and main theatre entrance. The partially fritted, faceted glass entrance lobby and gathering space contrasts with, and consciously subverts, the mass of the body of the building.

When approaching the site from the east along the mass to a drop-off point, the entry to the theatre is a sequential horizontal/vertical ascent. As the visitor climbs from the level plain of the high desert into the space of the lobby, soft northern light refracts through the angular glass to create shimmering geometric effects on the limestone walls and floor. A laminated cracked-glass balustrade defines the vertical ascent of the ceremonial stairs and upper lobby edge. Laminated cracked glass has also been used for pivoting panels, which give the option of greater privacy to the intimate theatre club on the upper level. The exterior gathering space on the upper level reorientates to the east. A recessed exterior stage platform at the west end of the structure focuses on a geometric garden. An all-weather entrance or covered drop-off zone penetrates the wedge north to south.

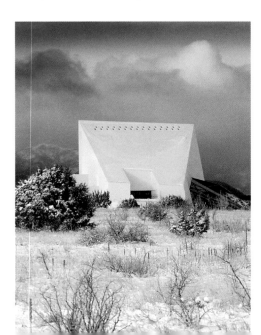

Opposite above The theatre's
limestone mass makes it almost
indistinguishable from its mountainous
surroundings in the snow. **Opposite
below** The end of the wedge-like form
of the theatre appears as if it has been
chiselled in a single blow. **Above** The
glowing lobby appears to erupt from the
limestone mass. **Right** The glass
faceted entrance lobby contains the
ceremonial stairs and upper lobby. The
glacial appearance of the structure
plays with the metaphor of the theatre
as a mountainous outcrop.

*Coloured fields caught in
cruciforms of steel tint the
desert "Mondrian" that
Wendell Burnette has built for
himself and his family in the
Sonoran desert..
Aaron Betsky.*[1]

This house, which was built by the architect for his wife and family, is an assertion of the architect's own architectural values. Wendell Burnette, who trained at Taliesin West for three years, strongly believes that to work in the tradition of Frank Lloyd Wright is to follow an innovative and modern impulse, rather than be imitative. In this house he uses basic commercial construction materials – such as masonry, steel, concrete and glass – but transforms them by his attention to detail. The most dominant feature is the outside walls, which appear as monoliths, framing the glass-faced rooms that reveal themselves as colourful interior compositions looking on to the desert. (The living–dining room is furnished in highly coloured modern furniture and the house is floodlit at night with primary colours.) The rooms are lined with the wooden formwork used for the pour-in-place concrete.

What really marks out Burnette's philosophy, however, is the way he has used the house in a poetic way to heal an ugly corner in a dense neighbourhood of late 1950s to early 1970s ranch-style houses, which marred the sensitive ecosystem of the desert. Discussing the concept of the house, Burnette refers to the site, a disused road, as a scar: 'The design solution is a band-aid for the scar; a man-made canyon that renders the surrounding neighbourhood less visible; focusing the view and creating a sense

of isolation with the desert mountains to the east. An internal court allows natural light to penetrate the 92-foot [28-metre] bar, providing a moment of focus within the canyon. From the auto and pedestrian entry, the internal garden is the focus, an oasis of light, shade and water, a slot to the sky which once climbs up through the reach to the separate interior volumes and the outdoor living spaces that lie above and below."[2]

It is through its truly contemporary understanding of its environment that the house distinguishes itself. The design has to cater for both the extreme conditions of the desert and man's destructive effect on the landscape (although positioned on the west face of the Phoenix Mountain Preserve, it is surrounded by housing). The interior panels, for instance, not only have slots between them so that they chart the movement of light around the house, but also serve to screen it from adjacent houses. In a combination of the pragmatic and the aesthetic, the internal climate is regulated by the inclusion of a shaded evaporative pool below the studio floor; water from the pool runs down the slope of the site into the internal courtyard. Auto-tint film technology has been used to maintain privacy, and to regulate light. The colourful floolights also allow the exterior of the house to become, using Betsky's analogy, the subject of the 'Mondrian' by night.

Wendell Burnette
Burnette Studio/House
Sunnyslope, Arizona, 1995

1 Aaron Betsky, 'House Hovers Over Desert Site', *Architectural Record*, April 1996, p94.
2 From a description provided by the architect's office in May 1998.

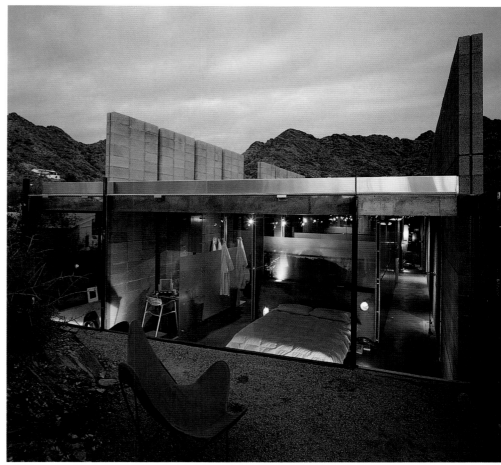

Opposite above Looking east from
the living—dining room. The slit concrete
panels on the north and south walls
filter the desert sun. **Opposite below**
The south terrace, which looks as
though it has been been created by a
concrete panel being pulled out of the
house's external wall. **Top** The entrance
court at the east front of the house.
Above left The kitchen. **Above right**
The parents' bedroom at the the rear of
house. **Right** Long section showing
the living block on the left and the
bedroom—studio block on the right.
The evaporative pool is situated
below the studio floor.

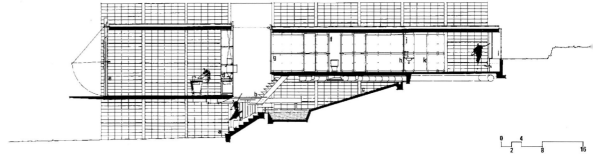

landscape, here the site for the projected house is wild and beautiful. Although the structural and sculptural base of the residence is to be formed out of the foundations and basement of an existing building, it is to be mounted on a piece of slick rock that to the east forms a sheer cliff face of Stone Canyon. Camelback Mountain will create the backdrop of the house, while above the red cliffs of Camel Head will loom.

The house will comprise two volumes, both worked into the landscape in the manner of modern outcrops. Generated out of a square footprint, the western volume (the 'private' side of the house) is to appear as if it has grown out of the existing basement foundation and taken root in the slick rock. The 'public' volume to the east is to float horizontally above the slick rock and beyond the east edge of the cliff. Juxtaposed as two independent solids, they are set apart by a canyon of light. This transparent glazed space provides the entrance to the underside of the public volume.

It is in his use of materials that Burnette is at his most ingenious. The volumes are to be covered with panels of mill-finish steel, evoking the black-brown patina of the volcanic rock in Stone Canyon. This echoes the contrasts that can be found in the natural geology of Camelback Mountain, with its 'black-brown' tones set against the redness of the slick rock.

The design for this residence, produced in response to the clients' wishes for a house that would constitute 'modern sculpture', develops many of the preoccupations that were apparent in Burnette's own house and studio. Here, however, the architect's emphasis on – and understanding of – a 'sense of place', is taken to a new height. Whereas in the Burnette Studio/House he was patching a scarred

Wendell Burnette
Nichols Residence
Paradise Valley, Arizona, 1998

Opposite above Computer rendering
of the south elevation, showing the
private volume of the house to the left
and the public volume to the right.
Opposite below A site montage
which displays the potential drama of
the house's location. **Above right**
Computer simulation of the interior of
the completed living room. **Above** Site
plan, mapping the mountainous terrain
surrounding the house. **Right** Computer
rendering of the main entrance, with
steps up to the house in foreground.

It is highly ironic that the new design paradigm, most often
referred to as 'new modernism', should be coming of age in 1990s Japan.
For although it first emerged in the mid to late 1980s, before the so-called Japanese 'bubble economy' burst,
it has come into full force in a period of restricted
economic growth. The dominance of modernism and modern architecture
in the 1960s was linked inextricably with the 'Japanese economic miracle',
and the unprecedented industrial boom that led to an ensuing
unchecked urbanism. During the 1970s, the introduction of postmodernism into just about every
aspect of cultural life – art and architecture being at the forefront – had been hastened by the
slow-down in the economy and the worldwide energy crisis; this was further fuelled by a general
disillusionment in the redeeming capacity of modern industrial technology and society, and by the
breakdown of long-established value systems. By the 1980s, the onset of an accelerated commodity
culture and the beginning of a new type of urbanism had become apparent. This manifested itself in
the triumph of mass consumer society, and the rebounding of production and consumption, promoted
by the rapid spread of radically new information technologies and the overall penetration of the
media into everyday life.

The need for a new architectural paradigm emerged in the early 1990s, when the
euphoria which had accompanied Japan's apparently unlimited promise and optimism in the 1980s
came to an end. Although the sombre economic climate did not change the basic parameters on
which the Japanese economy operates – it has remained one of the largest consumer societies in the
world – it certainly put a break on its runaway and overheated 'machine'. In the 1990s, as the millennium draws to a close, the need for the re-evaluation of Japanese society and the course that its
architectural and urban culture may – or should – take, has persisted. Within the architectural profession, the necessary and important shift in attitude that began in the last decade still continues. For this
reason, 'new modernism' can be regarded as occupying a space between modernism and postmodernism, having assimilated much of what both have to offer.

Although much of the feverish construction activity of the 'bubble' years resulted,
perhaps unavoidably, in frivolous and too often inferior designs, it also yielded a vast number of outstanding world-class projects; so much so that this period is often referred to as 'the new golden age
of Japanese architecture'. For quite some time, Japan has been playing an increasingly important role

Design in the Land of   *Botond Bognar*

'Creative Chaos'

The Emergence of New

Modernism in Japanese

Architecture

on the international design scene. Since the mid-1980s, the sheer volume of completed works (not to mention their outstanding quality) has matched and even surpassed the output of most other countries. Such exceptional projects include Fumihiko Maki's Fujisawa Gymnasium (1984), Spiral Building (1985) and Tokyo Metropolitan Gymnasia (1990); Kazuo Shinohara's TIT Centennial Hall (1987); Tadao Ando's Rokko Chapel (1986), Church on the Water (1988) and Church of Light (1989); Toyo Ito's Yatsushiro Municipal Museum (1991); Itsuko Hasegawa's Shonandai Cultural Center (1991); Hiroshi Hara's Yamato International Building (1987) and Iida City Museum (1988); and Shin Takamatsu's Kirin Plaza Building (1987). The list could go on and on.

    The success, while attributable to any number of forces — social and economic conditions, the availability of advanced technologies, the unusually high standard of the construction industry and its penchant for innovation, and the features of the physical and cultural environment of Japan — has also been closely tied to waves of talented Japanese architects. In addition to the long-standing national and international reputation of Kenzo Tange, the names of Arata Isozaki, Fumihiko Maki, Tadao Ando, Kisho Kurokawa, Kazuo Shinohara, Toyo Ito, Itsuko Hasegawa, Hiroshi Hara, Shin Takamatsu and others have emerged and become well-known both at home and abroad. In addition to winning important international competitions and foreign commissions, these architects have received distinguished international awards; Maki and Ando were awarded the most prestigious Pritzker Prize in Architecture in 1993 and 1995 respectively.[1] Another generation of designers, including individuals as diverse as Yoshio Taniguchi, Kazuyo Sejima, Riken Yamamoto, Ryoji Suzuki, Hajime Yatsuka, Waro Kishi, Masaharu Takasaki, Akiko and Hiroshi Takahashi, has also emerged. In their own particular and often singular ways, these architects' varied approaches have formed an unusually broad design spectrum.

    The ability of the Japanese to promote a high-quality architectural culture on such a broad scale is remarkable. It is a feat that relatively few countries have been able to achieve in our age of globalization, multi-national economies and universal civilization. In his 1992 book *Modern Architecture: A Critical History*, Kenneth Frampton identifies Finland, France and Spain, alongside Japan, as being the best representatives of a rich, modern architectural culture today.[2] Japan has attained this position despite the vagaries of its prevailing chaotic urban conditions — or perhaps, in some ways, because of them. It could be argued that many of the innovative qualities of contemporary Japanese architecture stem from this inherent urban chaos. Indeed, architectural works, especially the

Previous page Hajime Yatsuka, Angelo Tarlazzi Building, Tokyo, 1987. Architects such as Yatsuka have begun to outwardly express the chaos and complexity of the Japanese city through their own architecture. The Tarlazzi Building has the sort of random composition of colliding elements which occur in a quickly changing or unregulated urban environment.
Above Hiroshi Hara, Iida City Museum, Iida, Nagano Prefecture, 1988. The fragmentary composition and jagged roofscape echo the rugged forms of the range of mountains that surround it.
Right Kazuo Shinohara, Centennial Hall, Tokyo Institute of Technology, 1987.

most outstanding ones, cannot be properly understood without grasping their profound, often ambiguous, relationship with the deeply heterogeneous and undeniably chaotic Japanese city, whose overwhelming presence Chris Fawcett properly referred to almost two decades ago as 'Japan the City'.[3]

While Japanese architects have shown an increasing capacity to deal with the vicissitudes of any given set of circumstances, or the excessively complex and contradictory context advanced by the society and the times in which they operate, they have also successfully combined innovative departures with critical gestures and poetic poignancy. Such practices can be traced back as early as the late 1950s and early 1960s, and have their roots in the middle of the nineteenth century when Japan, still a feudal country, embarked on a formidable and unprecedented task of modernization. Nevertheless, it was in the second part of the twentieth century when the probity of Japanese architects began to emerge with more force and conviction in the face of new challenges. With the postwar reconstruction accomplished, the preparatory work for the 1964 Olympic Games in Tokyo opened a new chapter in contemporary Japanese architecture and urbanism. Bolstered by the 'economic miracle' and spearheaded in the 1960s by the Metabolists, Japanese architects established a reputation for being able to build just about anything, even the 'unbuildable'.[4] As opposed to other avant-garde movements, such as Archigram or Superstudio in Europe (to which the Metabolists have been compared often), the Japanese not only managed to build, and build extensively, but also they did so with the most innovative technologies. Thus, in the best cases, they were able to realize futuristic theoretical models within the 'pragmatism of construction'. Unlike the rest of the world, where the drawing board or computer are the reserve of the explorational, in Japan the construction site was, and still is, the primary testing ground for new ideas in architecture.

Change and interchangeability The 1960s continued with renewed energy and optimism in the tradition of the Meiji Restoration of 1868, in which Tokyo became a laboratory for testing primarily Western urban models. Architects both within and beyond the Metabolist group envisioned new modes of development for the metropolis. Their numerous radically bold schemes, which all relied on some form of megastructure and the advanced industrial technology that was by then widely available in Japan, proposed new frontiers in city planning. These included building above the fabric of the existing city, and over the sea. However, in such endeavours one could already recognize the first signs of a new (post-) modern and, one might add, non-Western design paradigm.

Right Kazuyo Sejima, Platform 2, Yamanashi Prefecture, 1989. The insubstantial materiality and often radically informal minimalism of Sejima's buildings – best represented by her 'Platform' Houses – while blurring the distinction between reality and illusion, reveal the designer's advocation of the ephemeral and the phenomenal in architecture.

Among the many emerging ideas, the notions of change and interchangeability, which revealed affinities with certain tenets of Japanese Buddhism and traditional urbanism, were responsible for putting in place more flexible or dynamic modes of urbanism. These new models also set themselves up in opposition to the old 'master plan' paradigms. Metabolist architects such as Kiyonori Kikutake and Kisho Kurokawa recognized that certain elements in the built environment wear out or, due to technological progress, become obsolete much more quickly than others; these elements therefore need to be replaced more frequently. But the Metabolists could not reconcile the fact that the (technological) model of change that they were advocating was bound up in the growing consumerism of Japanese society and in its relentless cycles of fashion, circumstances which they – still purist moderns at heart – criticized and wished to avoid.[5]

Although Metabolism declined during the 1970s, the ephemeral conditions of the consumer-oriented Japanese city in the 1980s and early 1990s were particularly conducive to the type of more flexible urban architecture they had originally promoted. As the Japanese economy shifted back into top gear once more, it triggered the most rapid, far-reaching and in many ways 'free for all' developments. This 'change in overdrive' was greatly to affect the course of both architecture and urbanism, and the quality of urban life in Japan.

Besides the overheated economy, exorbitant land prices and the virtually all-encompassing process of commercialization, the most significant influence on Japanese architecture and the city at this time was a manifest shift of emphasis from the previously dominant industrial or 'hardware' technologies, towards those involving highly sophisticated electronics or 'software'. Indeed, Japanese architecture since the 1980s can be characterized by the wholesale penetration of information and media technologies. These new technologies, with their inherent 'fuzzy logic' and invisibility, are better able to create a world that appeals to human emotions and desires. As such, they can lead to an increased fascination with image and sensuality in architecture.

Earlier modern architects would have viewed such tendencies in a negative light, but this is not the case today. These developments, moreover, are not merely the result of the insidious workings of consumerist capitalism; they are also the product of the historically evolved predisposition of Tokyo's (or the Japanese city's) urban culture. In the Edo period (pre-1868 Tokyo) this was extensively shaped by the ethos of a 'floating world';[6] now it has been further defined by new intellectual movements and scientific discoveries such as chaos theories, the concept of fractals, progress in

Right Fumihiko Maki, Fujisawa Municipal Gymnasium, Fujisawa, 1984. In the composition of this large complex, Maki brings together disparate elements without synthesizing them into a unified and uniform whole. A deviation from the 'classical' norms of modernism, it responds better to the tempo of contemporary urban culture.

astronomy and space research, computer technology and molecular biology. These and other developments have expanded the horizon of human consciousness both in terms of the macro and the micro. Contemporary design, as a matter of course, is caught up in the events of today's accelerated and volatile (urban) life. In other words, while it is undeniable that Japan's unprecedentedly restless and chaotic urbanism has rendered the fate of architecture unpredictable (both literally and semantically), it has also opened up virtually unlimited possibilities. It has provided an irresistible impetus for the most innovative and experimental designs, which can often be characterized by their sense of both realism and fiction.

New modernism and the urban context Some basic positions can be detected among the divergent, even paradoxical, approaches that Japan's urbanism has elicited. The earlier modernist aversion to the 'disorder' of the Japanese city has been debunked and its messy vitality, flexibility and resilience discovered, along with its still surviving Asian urban traditions. There is a new understanding that the heterogeneous, volatile and chaotic conditions of the city can lend an altogether different kind of order to anarchy. This can be the source of not only destructive forces but also of creative energies, and even a new poetic inspiration. Most of new modernism's various strands are equally critical of the elitist or purist – and too often dogmatic – tenets of previous orthodox modernism. At the same time, however, the 'new modernist' architects remain committed to continuing modernism's constructional innovation, its exploration of available technologies and new materials, and its general sympathy with a non-representational or non-historicist language. To illustrate the differences between orthodox and new modernism in Japan, it is interesting to compare two recent designs with their earlier modernist counterparts.

A comparison between Fumihiko Maki's Fujisawa Municipal Gymnasia of 1984 and Kenzo Tange's Tokyo Olympic Gymnasia of twenty years earlier, amply reveals the extent to which Maki deviates from the compositional principles (and also, one might say, the metaphysics) of orthodox modernism. While both designs comprise two interconnected volumes, possess an overall curvilinear geometry, and take the tradition of high tectonic culture as their common point of departure, they articulate the overall architectural form in diametrically opposite ways.

Tange's design is a *tour de force* of compositional unity, wherein every element in a strict hierarchy supports a fully integrated and homogeneous totality. Maki's masterpiece, on the other

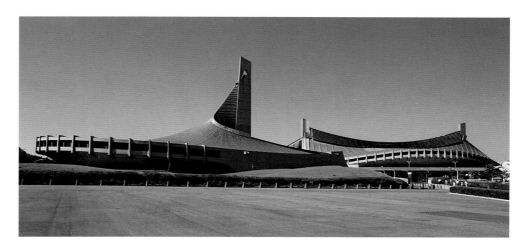

Right Kenzo Tange, Tokyo Olympic Gymnasia, Tokyo, 1964. Tange's stadia represented a watershed in Japanese architecture. After the political and economic upheavals of Japan's postwar years, the Olympics, which were seen worldwide on television, announced the country's arrival and acceptance back in the modern world. The resolution of the elliptical and circular steel roofs represented both the contemporary epitome of industry technology and the height of modernity.

hand, follows a fundamentally different sensibility. The design comprises two arenas, both of which differ not only in form and structure but also in their constituent elements and motives. Every vantage point of this fragmentary and collaged assemblage reveals an unexpected face, a new silhouette; in other words, each 'perspective' suggests another reading of the 'whole'. As a result, the Fujisawa Gym displays a perpetually shifting or, more precisely, perceptually 'unstable' and excitingly vibrant image. Moreover, due to the uniquely textured stainless-steel covered roofs, which glisten under certain light conditions, Maki's design attains a hallucinatory brilliance. In many ways it properly exemplifies and responds to its context: the dynamic but also fragmented landscape of the Japanese city.

In the words of Maki himself: 'The days when there was an immutable style … are past … The classical urban order having collapsed, any work of architecture that, in a sense, internalizes the city and functions on its exterior surface as a mechanism of [information] transmission will … symbolize today's image of the city – an environment that constantly renews its vitality precisely through its state of fragmentation.'[7] Such a mode of design, representing an integration without synthesis, is even more evident in Maki's subsequent works, for example in the highly sophisticated design of the Spiral Building in Tokyo (1985). Today these qualities are also apparent in the architecture of most other Japanese designers including Isozaki, Kurokawa, Shinohara, Takamatsu, Ito, Yamamoto and, most importantly, Ryoji Suzuki, Masaharu Takasaki and Hajime Yatsuka.

Another telling comparison illustrates differing attitudes towards the role of architecture in the contemporary city. Tange's New Tokyo City Hall (1991) and Shin Takamatsu's Kirin Plaza in Osaka (1987) demonstrate two diverging approaches to the monumental within the urban context. Tange, who has remained faithful to the classical urban design principles of orthodox modern architecture, favours a highly ordered urbanism; in this way he seeks to anchor an unimpeachable reality in the dizzyingly volatile realm of the city. The historicizing and rather dogmatic monumental design of his City Hall thus appears to represent a looming corporate totalitarianism: a model that is not only overly authoritarian, but which also presents itself in total opposition to the dynamics and resilient liveliness of the Japanese city.[8]

In contrast, Takamatsu's monumentalism is non-historicist, enigmatic and highly sensuous. His Kirin Plaza is the best example of this approach. It embodies the aesthetic of mysterious, precision-crafted and over-scaled mechanical models combined with the images of exhausted or 'dead' machines (or, rather, ritualistic objects). Intense in their expression, this and other buildings by

Above Fumihiko Maki, Spiral Building, Tokyo, 1985. One of Maki's most sophisticated designs, the Spiral Building is a layered collage of elements with multiple references, including old and new, modern and traditional, Western and Japanese.
Right Shin Takamatsu, Kirin Plaza, Osaka, 1987. It is in the pursuit of the monumental that the experiences of the post-modern period are most apparent. Work such as Takamatsu's diverges from the contained classical principles of 1960s modernism and recasts itself in a more fantastic and enigmatic direction.

Takamatsu appear as 'desiring instruments' for the rituals of today's urban life – a life in which, paradoxically, the traditional objects of worship have now been lost. Like hollowed-out and fragmented
empty shells deprived of any possible destination, Takamatsu's designs, despite their critical intentions, reinforce rather than oppose the frenzied new Japanese environment. This environment, as
Chris Fawcett has noted, 'by virtue of its ecstatic and delirious dreams of itself … is both a positive
affirmation and consumption of the Japanese metropolitan project'.[9]

Tange's somewhat pretentious and Takamatsu's highly sensuous (although void
and 'empty') views of monumentalism can be contrasted with that forwarded by Kazuo Shinohara in
his masterful Centennial Hall of the Tokyo Institute of Technology (1987). Here, incongruous and 'broken' structures, tortured forms and details comprise a design vocabulary that while in itself does not
seem to formulate a coherent statement, in its urban context of 'progressive anarchy' begins to make
sense. The building's many apparently accidental forms are the result of Shinohara's unique design
sensibility, which is capable of deciphering the unpredictable nexus of Tokyo's urban relationships and
events. His design concept for the Centennial Hall is what he refers to as a 'zero degree machine'. This
manifests itself in both a 'deconstruction' of the mechanical model of orthodox modern architecture,
and in its transformation into a new design paradigm of bewitching power.

The ephemeral and the phenomenal At the other end of the design spectrum, in terms of their
architectural intentions, are those architects who question the validity and even the possibility of mon-
umentality today, and experiment with the 'phenomenal' – the realm of the senses – and the
ephemeral. Rather than strive for monumental permanence, a growing number of architects have
begun to foster new urban sensibilities that favour ambiguity and perceptual instability, with an implicit
indeterminacy of meaning. In doing so they have often brought into play the evocative, and provocative, forces of nature and natural phenomena.

Perhaps the most distinguished practitioner in this area is Tadao Ando. From the
very beginning of his career he has pursued a line of modern design which is not only 'minimalist' and
provocative, but also displays an extreme sensitivity towards nature and the landscape. Opposed to
the 'indiscriminate' openness of orthodox modernism, and the modern world, Ando's works act as primarily inwardly oriented microcosms. Here, even nature is internalized, while being transformed
through the architecture itself. 'I suppose it could be said that my approach applies the vocabulary and

Right Shin Takamatsu, perspective of
Kunibiki Messe and Convention Centre,
Matsue City, 1993. Kunibiki Messe is
a demonstration of the success of the
monumental in recent architecture.
The Japanese are able to build on a
vast scale, accommodating a large
number of people in one complex,
and create a variety of spaces which
maintain human proportions. Less
stylized than Takamatsu's earlier Kirin
Plaza (opposite), the Kunibiki Messe
uses light to break down the large
volumes of the building's mass
(see pp124–5).

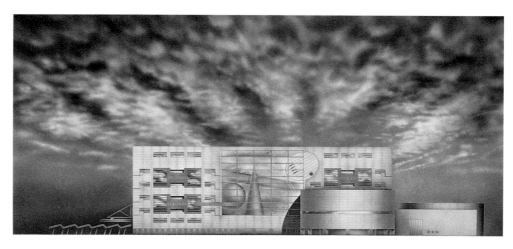

techniques developed by an open, universal modernism within the enclosed realm of individual lifestyles and regional conventions,' says Ando. 'What I refer to as enclosed modern architecture is a restoration of the unity between house and nature, which Japanese houses have lost in the process of modernization … I attempt to choose from the forces latent in a particular region where I am working, and this way to develop a theory … that is founded on the sensibilities of the Japanese people.'[110] Ando uses the concrete wall – perhaps his most important design element – as a device with which to layer space and passages in an intricate way. He also uses its increasingly luxurious surfaces as a base on to which the changing phenomena of nature, and the events of daily life, can be projected and captured – like a delicate screen. Ando's poetically evocative designs, with their magical light-and-shadow effects, are now legendary.

Continuing his interest and artistry in choreographing architectural spaces and mobilizing natural phenomena in buildings of unfinished concrete, Tadao Ando in the 1990s has expanded his repertoire by successfully transcribing many of the features of his earlier designs into larger, public and even commercial or fashion complexes. This is indicative of a change in attitude which is apparent among many other Japanese architects. Ando's previously explicitly negative stance towards the city has been attenuated, though he has not altogether abandoned an implicitly critical position. Therefore, although his characteristic interior courtyard arrangement reappears in various configurations in many of his urban projects, it is now articulated so as to assure somewhat more open overall spatial compositions than before. In other words, Ando's new architecture engages both the natural and the built environment more actively, although still selectively.

In addition to a growing number of younger designers who, like Ando, explore the phenomenal in architecture, Yoshio Taniguchi has emerged both at home and on the international scene as one of the most important Japanese architects in the 1990s. His crisp and remarkably elegant modern designs, while unfailingly capturing the poetic effects of light and water, have been particularly successful in engendering a new urban architecture. Taniguchi's Marugame Genichiro Inokuma Museum of Contemporary Art (1991) features, under the canopy of its roof, a large and cavernous open atrium as well as a wide stairway. Both serve to continue the public space of the urban plaza in front, but within the fabric of the building itself. Today, not only individual atelier-type architects but also large design companies, especially Nikken Sekkei Ltd and Takenaka Design, are leaving behind their reputation as designers largely of huge corporate office buildings, and are increasingly turning

Above Yoshio Taniguchi, Genichiro Inokuma Museum of Contemporary Art, Marugame, Kagawa Prefecture, 1991. The themes of water and light are as important to Taniguchi as to Tadao Ando (right). This museum introduces light by means of a large central atrium.
Right Tadao Ando, Water Temple, Higashiura-cho (Awaji Island), Hyogo Prefecture, 1991. Ando is famous for having imbued modern architecture with a new sense of calm and spirituality. This temple was built for the Shingon Buddhist sect. The temple hall is underground, below the oval pond filled with lotus plants.

Right Nikken Sekkei Ltd, Nasu Konami Employee Training Center, Nasu, Ibaraki Prefecture, 1994. A growing number of projects by Nikken Sekkei Ltd, the largest firm in Japan, not only continue to be beautifully crafted pieces of architecture, but are also designed as spectacular sequences of spaces that often engage in changes taking place in nature and human life.
Below Toyo Ito, Nagaoka Lyric Hall, Niigata Prefecture, 1996. Ito's Lyric Hall, with its emphasis on the flow of space rather than the rigid rational architecture of the 1960s epitomizes contemporary architecture in Japan. This cross-section shows how the auditoria and separate spaces of the hall are unified under a single undulating roof, creating one continuous form rather than a series of volumes.

out highly sophisticated projects. These have included such masterpieces as Nikken's Nasu Konami Employee Training Center (1994) and Takenaka's R-90 Research and Development Center (1993).

Although Ando and many others mainly use reinforced concrete for their architecture, in recent years designers have increasingly adopted lighter, usually high-tech industrial materials, such as perforated aluminum, stainless steel, Teflon fibre, new kinds of glass — such as LC glass and fibreglass — and polycarbon membranes. The resulting structures, by virtue of their lack of heavy materiality and their often fragmentary compositions, are intended to form part of the changing environment rather than be dominant, permanent objects with deterministic forms. In a characteristically Japanese way, boundaries are frequently defined without being rigidly established. Spaces are wrapped in multiple layers of screens and other thin membrane-like elements. These elements, as well as relying increasingly on lightweight and translucent or transparent materials, take advantage of the latest technologies in their display or operation, including lighting, lasers and various computer-controlled devices. New structural solutions and mastery of design have also helped create a feeling of phenomenal lightness, especially in the work of Maki.

The true antithesis to the monumental, however, is pursued by those architects whose designs are comprised of minimal material substance. In these cases, reality is constituted largely by the environment in which a structure is set, and which in turn gives it being. The 'essence' of these supremely lightweight structures is not only related to natural and/or human phenomena and

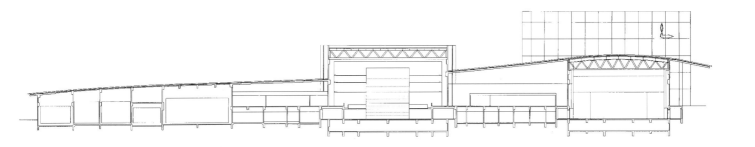

events, but is also, in effect, evoked by them. Taking the form of temporary shelters, many recent works by Toyo Ito, Kazuyo Sejima, Itsuko Hasegawa, Kazunari Sakamoto, Maki and others conjure up the ephemeral. This architecture aspires not only to perceptual but also to physical impermanence. It has brought about both a new 'industrial vernacular' and a new kind of space – which might be called 'imminent' space.[11] It is in this sense that most of Ito's and Hasegawa's projects, beginning with the Shonandai Cultural Center (1991), evoke the image of futuristic high-tech camps for today's 'urban nomads'.[12] Indeed, new materials and technologies, along with new modes of design, can now provide the possibility of constructing 'architecture' with an almost immaterial lightness and transparency. As metaphors, lightness and transparency are the manifestations of a new understanding of the world as being in a state of flux, a world whose order of 'creative chaos' can only be approached by a new, 'modal' consciousness, which is unfettered by the stable conception or the rigid, one-point perspectival view of the world.

Blueprint for a new modernism Today's evolving new modernism, in Japan, manifests itself in lightness, in fragmentation, in 'dissolution' and in the increased significance of surfaces. Other important aspects of the paradigm are the new roles of technology, high-tech craftsmanship, 'imageability', sensuousness and a spectacular 'aperspective' phenomenalism. We also see a renewed concern for nature and the environment, and the reinterpretation of the notion of 'place' as an active and continuously shifting condition, derived from often unpredictable events rather than permanent qualities.

The critic Ignasi de Solá-Morales has summed up this new atmosphere of impermanence: 'The places of present-day architecture cannot repeat the permanencies produced by the force of the Vitruvian *firmitas*. The effects of duration, stability, and defiance of time's passing are now irrelevant. The idea of place as the cultivation and maintenance of the essential and the profound, of a *genius loci*, is no longer credible in an age of agnosticism; it becomes reactionary.'[13] He identifies a new way forward for architecture in this shifting world: 'The loss of these illusions need not necessarily result in a nihilistic architecture of negation. From a thousand different sites the production of place continues to be possible. Not as a revelation of something existing in permanence, but as the production of an event.'[14]

On the other hand, despite such theories and the individual efforts of many architects, it is also increasingly apparent that a clearly defined critical practice has become a near impossibility

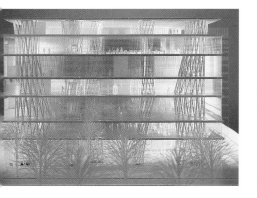

Above Toyo Ito, computer rendering for Mediatheque Library, Sendai, to be completed in 2000. An important strand in today's modernism is a preoccupation with light and ephemeral structures, which reflect the transitory nature of Japanese city life.

1 The third Japanese architect, Kenzo Tange, received the Pritzker Prize in 1987.
2 Kenneth Frampton, *Modern Architecture: A Critical History*, Thames and Hudson (New York), 1992, pp331–43.
3 Chris Fawcett, *The New Japanese House*, Harper and Row (New York), 1980, p24. Japan is one of the world's most crowded and urbanized countries; some 123 million people live on an island the size of California, but only thirty per cent of this area is inhabitable, or can be used for agriculture, industry and so on; the rest is excessively moutainous with many volcanoes. This fact prompted Fawcett to call the whole of Japan a 'city'.
4 Kenneth Frampton, 'On Nikken Sekkei,' in B Bognar, K Frampton, S Heck, *Nikken Sekkei: Building Modern Japan 1900–1990*, Princeton Architectural Press (New York), 1990, p11.
5 The rapid advancement of technology makes most industrial products obsolete in shorter and shorter periods of time, fostering a need of their cyclical replacement, which is similar to changes in fashion, and other cycles of consumption.
6 The 'floating world' or *ukiyoe* refers to the spirit of Edo culture, essentially a culture of merchants and artisans

within the the Japanese city's accelerated, simulated and ephemeral world. In Masao Miyoshi and Harry D Harootunian's opinion, 'the nation's critical and intellectual space is now painlessly absorbed into its productive space, calming the discontented and silencing all the dissenters.'[15] In other words, a critical practice in architecture has to be, and indeed tends to be, implicated or absorbed in the very processes it intends to oppose, or at least keep in check. Maintaining a critical position, therefore, may mean pursuing a practice which, while still at odds with both technological domination and rampant consumerism, acknowledges their modus operandi as the only remaining alternative to create architectural (and perhaps also urban) renewal.

This much is clear from the words of Toyo Ito, who more than others realizes that architects cannot really isolate themselves from society: 'I believe architecture [today] must reflect the city called Tokyo. Right now [in the Japanese city] life and architecture itself are gradually losing their reality. They are not down-to-earth. I often use the word "floating" not only to describe the lightness I want to achieve in architecture, but also to express a belief that our lives are losing touch with reality. All of life is becoming a pseudo-experience. This trend is being encouraged by the consumer society, and architecture itself is rapidly becoming more image – or consumption – oriented.'[16] Ito reacts to this with a combination of resignation and pragmatism, but also with the curiosity of an explorer: 'This is a matter of grave concern to the architect yet, at the same time, architecture today must be made to relate to this situation. This is the contradiction we are confronted with … [Nevertheless] I do not want merely to reject this state of affairs; instead, I want to enter into this situation a bit further and to confirm what sort of architecture is possible [within it].'[17]

Ito's words, as much as the wide variety of recent Japanese architecture, reveal the complexity of issues and the dilemmas faced by architects today in Japan, and beyond. Economic and social, scientific and cultural, not to mention political developments in our accelerated age of information demand highly flexible and constantly shifting strategies. This is an attitude that acknowledges many tenets of both post-modernism and modernism, but is devoid of the fetish of the worn-out clichés of the former, as well as the rigid dogmas or false utopias of the latter; it is by nature exploratory and experimental. While in general terms one might say that new modernism establishes in innovative ways a feasible link between these two previous paradigms in architecture and urbanism, in the best cases this is not a 'simple' combination. As a growing number of Japanese designs demonstrate, it is a curious transcendence of both.

whose spirit peaked in the late seventeenth/early eighteenth century, and later in the early nineteenth. It can be characterized by two interrelated features, both of them important in shaping the prevailing urban culture: first, a certain hedonism, fuelled by a growing appreciation of Buddhist teachings about the 'transitoriness of life' and the 'evanescence of things'; and second, the pursuit of 'pleasures in everyday life'. The 'floating world' was also expressed in the popular arts, particularly the wood-block prints of the era.

7 Fumihiko Maki, 'Spiral', JA, The Japan Architect, March 1987, p33.

8 Tange's design for the City Hall, with its two interconnected towers, has been often criticized as one which is modelled on medieval French cathedrals, such as Notre Dame in Paris.

9 Chris Fawcett, The New Japanese House, Harper and Row (New York), 1980, p24.

10 Tadao Ando, 'From Self-Enclosed Modern Architecture towards Universality', JA, The Japan Architect (301), May 1982, p8.

11 Actually, during the 'bubble economy' many buildings were designed as solely temporary structures, which, after a period of few years, were demolished

and replaced with something more profitable. Some of them, like Toyo Ito's Nomad Restaurant (1986), or Masaharu' Takasaki's Crystal Light (1986), both in Tokyo, existed merely for two or three years.

12 Toyo Ito, in an interview with Sophie Roulet and Sophie Soulie, entitled 'Towards a Post-ephemeral Architecture', in Sophie Roulet and Sophie Soulie (eds), Toyo Ito, Editions du Moniteur (Paris), 1991, pp96–7.

13 Ignasi de Solá-Morales, Differences., quoted in Harvard Design Magazine, Fall 1997, p2.

14 Ibid.

15 Masao Miyoshi and Harry D

Harootunian (eds), Postmodernism and Japan, Duke University Press (Durham, NC), 1989, pXI.

16 Toyo Ito, 'Shinjuku Simulated City', in JA, The Japan Architect, 3/1991, p51.

17 Ibid.

This museum is devoted to the research and exhibition of the burial mound (*kofun*) culture of Japan (AD 300–538). It is situated in the southern part of Osaka Prefecture, which was the cradle of Japanese civilization during this period, and where there are more than two hundred burial mounds, including four imperial tombs. The museum serves both as an exhibition centre for unearthed objects and as an observation point for looking at the large number of mounds scattered in the immediate area.

Ando's design features an extensive system of stairs that span the entire width of the rooftop. The huge reinforced concrete structure thus seems to emerge from the earth below; the building was conceived as a manmade hill that would both blend in with and highlight its natural, wooded environment. Topped with an additional tower, the stepped roof is also designed to be used for various outdoor activities such as festivals, performances and lectures. At the same time, much of the museum's interior remains underground, making it evocative of the atmosphere of the inside of a large and dark *kofun*. Like many of Ando's designs of the 1990s, the Chikatsu-Asuka Historical Museum uses earth as an architectural element to spectacular effect.

Tadao Ando
Chikatsu-Asuka
Historical Museum
Kawachi, Osaka Prefecture, 1994

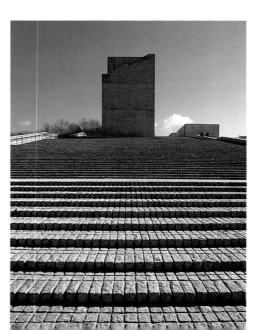

Opposite above The cavernous interior of the museum has a tomb-like atmosphere. There are no windows in the side walls, the only natural light source is a skylight over a multistorey central 'atrium'. **Opposite below** View of stepped roof looking up towards the tower. **Above** The museum's system of stairs is its defining feature. They extend up the side and over the front of the building. **Right** Longitudinal section showing the extensive stepped roof of the museum, leading to the observation platform on top and tower at the centre. The exhibition spaces beneath can also be seen centred around and under the dark void of the tower.

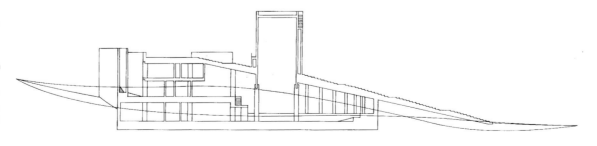

Occupying two city blocks in a satellite town of Tokyo, the centre is a project on a truly urban scale and one of the largest works to date by Hasegawa. It is also one of the most remarkable designs to be completed in the early 1990s. The scheme features a children's museum, workshops, galleries and practice rooms; a civic theatre (in the large globe); a space theatre (in the small globe); and an open-air theatre, together with associated services. At the top of the building there is an intricate outdoor promenade with terraces, bridges, ramps and stairways.

With its various elements, the centre is designed as a small urban community around a public plaza and playground. This forms the 'rooftop', below which are underground spaces, exhibition halls and a car park. In addition to the two large and one smaller spherical volumes, Hasegawa designed numerous tiny pyramid-like roofs and canopies, all of which are shaped in or wrapped with stainless steel and highly polished aluminium. The plaza is highlighted by a stream of water and a pool, small bridges, artificial 'trees' of metallic screens and a unique clockwork sculpture that performs an audio-visual show every hour.

The image is both futuristic and vernacular, even 'natural' – at least in Hasegawa's sense of the word. In her recent designs Hasegawa has aimed to redefine

architecture as 'another nature'. This has led not only to allusions to natural forms or the evocation of natural elements, but also to the provision of ample space and the opportunity for the natural world itself to penetrate and interact with the architecture – often with spectacular results.

The Shonandai Center, with its subtle and fragmentary qualities, is able to continue the heterogeneous, collage-like texture of the surrounding city yet, by way of both 'primitivism' and the application of technological details and solutions, it also substantially redefines the same environment. The project, thus, is the outcome of a paradoxical design strategy, in which the forces of both simulation and dissimulation act together.

Itsuko Hasegawa
Shonandai Cultural Center
Fujisawa, Kamagawa
Prefecture, 1991

Opposite above Evening view of the rooftop plaza with pool and canopies.
Opposite below The canopies over the plaza. **Above** Macro- and microcosmic landscapes, evoked by the numerous surrounding metallic elements and forms and small stream of water, define the futuristic and also 'primitively' vernacular central plaza.
Right Long section, showing the plaza with various roofs and canopies to the left, the space theatre in the small dome in the centre, and the civic theatre in the large dome to the left. The exhibition halls and a car park are accommodated underground.

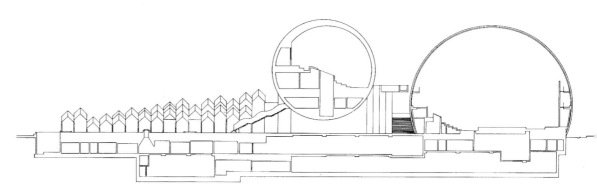

The Nagaoka Lyric Hall is a continuation of the design paradigm that Toyo Ito has been developing in his work throughout the 1990s. By setting out to create flowing space, it contrasts sharply with the rigidly rectangular (and rational) architecture of mid-twentieth-century modernism.

The paradigm expresses itself in the large complex in several ways. Located on the outskirts of Nagaoka City, the hall is largely defined by its thin, long, softly undulating roof membrane, which echoes the vastness of the surrounding scenery with its rolling hills and mountains. The architect has also landscaped much of the immediately surrounding area so that it undulates gently, making the new structure appear as a direct continuation of the land in which it is set. This use of the land as an architectural element has been a feature of Ito's work for some time.

The roof in Nagaoka is an important element in shaping the interiors of the hall; it appears, like a wind-blown tent or canvas, floating above the gently flowing spaces beneath, which surround the more enclosed volumes of the two auditoria: a 700-seat concert hall and a 450-seat theatre. With the enclosing, undulating boundaries of the building defined by full-height glazing, the distinction between the inside and the outside is ambiguous. The ambience is one of profound lightness. The roof is also punctuated by several round or oval openings, thus creating inner courtyards or roof-lights, which introduce rays of light into the fabric of the structure. Furthermore, with the pillars inside arranged in a seemingly random fashion, the overall effect, in Ito's words, is to provide 'the atmosphere of being in a forest'.

Ito has designed the concert hall with a translucent and corrugated-glass screen, which envelops the oval walls outside and protects the inside from the noise of the bypass road to the north of the site. In the evening, this luminous membrane is lit from behind and the glowing volume transforms the hall into a phenomenal landmark. The special use of artificial light is also a feature of the interior; the pipe organ and 'stage' of the concert hall, for example, are surrounded by a row of vertical glass-fibre rods, which are illuminated with various intensities from below, providing a soft but vibrant curtain of light before and during performances.

While benefiting from several of Ito's earlier design elements and strategies, the Nagaoka Lyric Hall also foreshadows the direction of his more recent projects . The Ota District Community Resort Complex in Nagano (1998) and the Sendai Mediatheque (due for completion in 2001) are even more substantial realizations of the phenomenal lightness of Toyo Ito's work.

Toyo Ito
Nagaoka Lyric Hall
Nagaoka, Niigata Prefecture, 1996

Opposite above Even while still under construction filterd soft light animated the flowing spaces of the extensive lobby. **Opposite below** The overhanging light-roof structure creates an ambiguous border between inside and outside. **Above** The long, softly undulating membrane of the roof seems to float above the equally wavy topos of the surrounding landscape, while also succeeding in unifying the architectural elements that are below and penetrating it. **Right** The interior of the large concert hall is accentuated by the warm artificial lighting that includes a system of vertical glass fibre 'rods' behind the stage.

Completed some twenty-six years after Kenzo Tange's famous Olympic Gymnasia, and not very far from them in location, Maki's scheme shows an interesting contrast with its earlier counterpart, while matching it in its architectural achievements. Replacing the outdated and inadequate previous facilities, the new Tokyo Metropolitan Gym provides more amenities for a greater number of people. The main arena seats ten thousand and the swimming pool nine hundred; additional structures accommodate a training hall, large entrance hall and administrative offices. The whole complex, which also includes an open-air athletics field with running tracks, is connected beneath an attractive, slightly elevated urban plaza.

Maki's design greatly differs to those of Tange in its loose, 'collaged' composition, in which the unity of the whole is challenged by the individuality of its constituent parts. The multiplicity of tilting, contracting and dilating arches, sensuously curving lines and a system of more streamlined shell surfaces reveal a design sensibility that departs from the established norms of high modernism. This large urban complex is an attempt to better address the heterogeneous quality of Tokyo, without compromising the structural/constructional requirements involved. In fact, here, Maki has been able to second the spectacular achievements represented by his Fujisawa Gym of 1984; in Tokyo, he has repeated on an even bigger scale the unique structural design of the large space arena, using only curvilinear elements, such as girders and frames, whose articulation greatly contributes to the arresting appearance of the structure. Like its predecessor in Fujisawa, the Tokyo Gym is also covered with stainless-steel sheets. This imbues the entire volume with a certain lightness and 'floating' quality.

Fumihiko Maki
Tokyo Metropolitan Gymnasium
Tokyo, 1990

Opposite above Interior of the large
arena, looking up to the spectacular
roof with its curvilinear girders and
frames. **Opposite below** Underside of
the exterior wall. **Above** The stainless-
steel clad panelled shell of the main
arena creates a helmet-like form.
Right Cross section of the main arena
showing the complex roof structure.

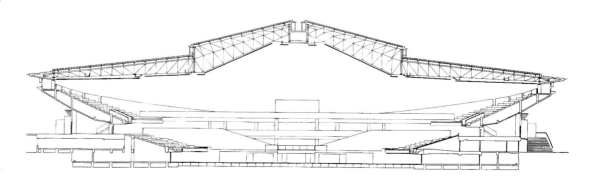

During the early 1990s, Takamatsu's work began to show signs of a new design approach. Prompted by the increasing scale of his commissions and a new, more expansive design sensibility, many of his growing number of projects have started to feature large, 'transparent' and light-filled spaces. These are less agitated by the sort of excessive detailing that was so apparent in Kirin Plaza, Osaka (1987). The Kunibiki project is the most spectacular proof of the success of this new direction. The large building with a total floor area of 15,700 square metres (168,900 feet) is both a venue for conferences and trade fairs, and the administrative centre for various prefectural organizations.

    The basic composition distinguishes these two functions in its form. It comprises two adjoining simple rectangular volumes: a horizontal one for exhibitions, and a vertical one for offices. Two additional cylindrical volumes contain multi-purpose spaces. The entire structure is shaped and/or wrapped in ferrous panels and other high-tech materials. Steel framed, much of it is covered in stainless-steel and aluminum plates. The meticulously executed metallic surfaces of the facades are interrupted by specially designed flush-mounted glass windows.

    The most astonishing part of the design, and the highlight of Takamatsu's project,

is a 24-metre (78-foot) high atrium within the vertical block. Enclosed in-between two large glass walls, this ethereal space features numerous geometric solids with metallic surfaces 'floating' within it. These volumes – cones, a globe, a horizontal oval cylinder and a slanting glass tube, all of which contain extra spaces within the larger one – are constructed with the utmost precision and with the sensuality and 'coolness' of space-age technology. Referred to as the 'Garden of Abstract Forms' by Takamatsu this atrium contributes greatly to the overall science-fiction quality of the architecture. At night, Kunibiki Messe is as spectacular as it is by day when light is reflected off, and also emitted through, its delicate surfaces.

Shin Takamatsu
Kunibiki Messe and
Convention Center
Matsue, Shimane Prefecture, 1993

Opposite above The top of the cone in the high atrium, or 'Garden of Abstract Forms', within the rectangular vertical office block. **Opposite below** Interior view of the multi-purpose space. **Above left** Glass corridor. **Above right** Cluster of cones in the 'Garden of Abstract Forms' **Left** The 'Garden of Abstract Forms' seen from the exterior.

Bibliography

General

Berman Marshall, *All That Is Solid Melts Into Air: The Experience of Modernity*, Penguin (Harmondsworth, Middlesex), 1988.

Borden Iain and David Dunster (eds), *Architecture and the Sites of History: Interpretations of Buildings and Cities*, Butterworth Architecture (Oxford), 1995.

Borden Iain, Joe Kerr, Alicia Pivaro and Jane Rendell (eds), *Strangely Familiar: Narratives of Architecture in the City*, Routledge (London), 1996.

Coates Nigel, 'Brief Encounters', in Iain Borden, Joe Kerr, Jane Rendell and Alicia Pivaro (eds), *The Unknown City: Contesting Architecture and Social Space* (forthcoming).

Dreysse DW, *Ernst May Housing Estates: Architectural Guide to Eight New Frankfort [sic] Estates (1926–1930)*, Fricke Verlag (Frankfurt), 1988.

Ellin Nan, *Postmodern Urbanism* Blackwel (Oxford), 1996.

— (ed), *Architecture of Fear*, Princeton Architectural Press (New York), 1997.

Fishman Robert, *Urban Utopias in the Twentieth Century: Ebenezer Howard, Frank Lloyd Wright and Le Corbusier*: MIT (Cambridge, Mass), 1982.

Frampton Kenneth, *Modern Architecture: A Critical History*, Thames and Hudson (London), 1980.

Ghirardo Diane, *Architecture After Modernism*, Thames and Hudson (London), 1996.

— *Building New Communities: New Deal America and Fascist Italy*, Princeton University Press (Princeton), 1989.

— (ed), *Out of Site: A Social Criticism of Architecture*, Bay Press (Seattle), 1991.

Gottdiener Mark, *Postmodern Semiotics: Material Culture and the Forms of Postmodern Life*, Blackwell (Oxford), 1995.

Harvey David, *Justice, Nature and the Geography of Difference*, Blackwell (Oxford), 1996.

Hertzberger Herman, 'The Public Realm', *Architecture and Urbanism*, April 1991, pp12–45.

Hill Jonathan (ed), *Occupying Architecture: Between the Architect and the User*, Routledge (London), 1998.

Hitchcock Henry Russell and Philip Johnson, *The International Style: Architecture Since 1922*, WW Norton & Company (New York and London), 1932; the 1966 paperback edition was simply entitled *The International Style*.

Jencks Charles, *The Language of Post-Modern Architecture*, Academy Editions and Rizzoli (London and New York), 1977.

— *Late-Modern and Other Essays*, Rizzoli (New York), 1980.

— (ed), *Post-Modern Classicism, The New Synthesis*, *Architectural Design* Academy Editions (London), 1980.

Jencks Charles and Karl Kropf (eds), *Theories and Manifestoes of Contemporary Architecture*, Academy Editions (London), 1997.

King Ross, *Emancipating Space: Geography, Architecture and Urban Design*, Guilford (New York), 1996.

Lefebvre Henri, *Introduction to Modernity: Twelve Preludes September 1959–May 1961*, Verso (London), 1995.

Lefebvre Henri, *The Production of Space*, Blackwell (Oxford), 1991.

Miller Lane Barbara, *Architecture and Politics in Germany, 1918–1945*, Harvard University Press (Cambridge, Mass), 1985.

Nesbitt Kate (ed), *Theorizing a New Agenda for Architecture: An Anthology of Architectural Theory 1965–1995* Princeton Architectural Press (New York), 1996.

Ockman Joan (ed), *Architecture Culture 1943–1968*, Rizzoli (New York), 1993.

Ockman Joan, Deborah Berke and Mary McLeod (eds), *Architecture, Criticism, Ideology*, Princeton Architectural Press (Princeton), 1985.

Raeburn Michael and Victoria Wilson (eds), *Le Corbusier: Architect of the Century*, Arts Council of Great Britain (London), 1987.

Sanders Joel (ed), *Stud: Architectures of Masculinity*, Princeton Architectural Press (Princeton), 1996.

Sassen Saskia, *The Global City: New York, London, Tokyo*, Princeton University Press (Princeton), 1991.

Tafuri Manfredo, *Architecture and Utopia*, MIT (Cambridge, Mass), 1976.

Tafuri Manfredo, and Francesco Dal Co, *Modern Architecture, Vols 1 and 2* Faber and Faber (London), 1986.

Tschumi Bernard, *Architecture and Disjunction*, MIT (Cambridge, Mass), 1996.

— 'Architecture and the City', in Iain Borden, Joe Kerr, Jane Rendell and Alicia Pivaro (eds), *The Unknown City: Contesting Architecture and Social Space* (forthcoming).

Wolfe Tom, *From Bauhaus to Our House*, Picador (London), 1993.

Wright Frank Lloyd, *The Living City* Horizon (New York), 1958.

Britain

Cook Peter (ed), *Archigram*, Studio Vista (London), 1972.

Esher Lionel, *A Broken Wave: The Rebuilding of England 1940–1980*, Allen Lane (London), 1981.

Forty Adrian, 'Being or Nothingness: Private Experience and Public Architecture in Post-War Britain', *Architectural History*, no 38, 1995, pp25–35.

Glendinning Miles and Stefan Muthesius, *Tower Block: Modern Public Housing in England, Scotland, Wales and Northern Ireland*, Yale University Press (London), 1994.

Gourlay Maureen, 'Paternoster Square and St Paul's: An Architectural Dilemma', MSc thesis for the Bartlett University College, London, 1997.

Hardingham Samantha, *England: A Guide to Recent Architecture*, Ellipsis (London), 1995.

Mort Frank, *Cultures of Consumption: Commerce, Masculinities and Social Space in Late Twentieth-Century Britain*, Routledge (London), 1996.

Pawley Martin, 'Future Systems', catalogue for exhibition at the ICA, London, 1 April–24 May 1998.

Rogers Richard, *Cities for a Small Planet*, Faber and Faber (London), 1997.

Rowe Colin, 'James Stirling: A Highly Personal and Very Disjointed Memoir', in Peter Arnell and Ted Bickford (eds), *James Stirling: Buildings and Projects*, The Architectural Press (London), 1984.

USA

Arnell Peter and Ted Bickford (eds), *Frank Gehry Buildings and Projects* Rizzoli (New York), 1985.

Arnold Joseph L, *The New Deal in the Suburbs: A History of the Greenbelt Town Program, 1935–1954*, The Ohio State University, Columbus, 1971.

Barr Alfred H Jr, Henry Russell Hitchcock, Philip Johnson and Lewis Mumford, *Modern Architects*, Museum of Modern Art and WW Norton & Company (New York), 1932, catalogue of the exhibition of the same name.

Bédard Jean-Francois, *Cities of Artificial Excavation, The Work of Peter Eisenman, 1978–1988*, Canadian Centre for Architecture (Montreal), 1994.

Drexler Arthur (ed), *Architecture of the Ecole des Beaux-Arts*, The Museum of Modern Art (Montreal), 1977, catalogue of the exhibition from 29 October 1975 to 4 January 1976.

Elderfield John (ed), *Imagining the Future of The Museum of Modern Art*, The Museum of Modern Art (New York), 1998.

Fitch James Marson, *American Building: The Environmental Forces that Shaped it*, Houghton Mifflin (Boston), 1947 and 1972.

Five Architects, Wittenborn & Company (New York), 1972.

Goldberger Paul, *The City Observed: New York*, Vintage Books (New York), 1979.

Jacobs Jane, *Death and Life of Great American Cities*, Vintage Books (New York), 1961.

Johnson Philip, 'Rejected Architects', *Creative Arts*, June 1931, pp433–5.

Johnson Philip and Mark Wigley, *Deconstructivist Architecture*, Little, Brown and Company (Boston), 1988, catalogue of the exhibition at The Museum of Modern Art, New York, 23 June–30 August 1988, curated by Johnson, catalogue essay by Wigley.

Plunz Richard, *A History of Housing in New York City*, Columbia University Press (New York), 1990.

Sorkin Michael, *Exquisite Corpse, Writing on Buildings*, Verso Books (London and New York), 1991.

— *Local Code, The Constitution of a City at 42° N Latitude*, Princeton Architectural Press (New York), 1993.

—, (ed) *Variations on a Theme Park: The New American City and the End of Public Space*, Noonsday Press (New York), 1992.

Stern Robert A M, Gregory Gilmartin, Thomas Mellins, *New York 1930: Architecture and Urbanism Between the Two World Wars*, Rizzoli (New York), 1987.

Stern Robert AM, Thomas Mellins, David Fishman, *New York 1960: Architecture and Urbanism Between the Second World Wars and the Bicentennial*, The Monacelli Press (New York), 1995.

Venturi Robert, *Complexity and Contradiction in Architecture*, The Museum of Modern Art Papers on Architecture (New York), 1966.

Willensky Elliot and Norval White, *AIA Guide to New York City*, Harcourt Brace Jovanovich (New York), 1988.

Japan

Bognar Botond, *The New Japanese Architecture*, Rizzoli (New York), 1990.

—, *The Japan Guide*, Princeton Architectural Press (New York), 1995.

—, 'What Goes Up, Must Come Down: Recent Urban Architecture in Japan,' *Durability and Ephemerality: Harvard Design Magazine*, Fall 1997, pp33–43.

—, 'The Other "End" of Architecture: The Japanese Example', *New Architecture* (London), No 2, October 1998.

— (ed), *Japanese Architecture, AD Profile No.73*, Academy Editions (London), 1988.

— (ed), *Japanese Architecture II, AD Profile No 99*, Academy Editions (London), 1992.

— (ed), *World Cities: Tokyo*, Academy Editions (London), 1997.

Coldrake William H, *Architecture and Authority in Japan*, Routledge (London), 1996.

Dal Co Francesco (ed), *Tadao Ando: Complete Works*, Phaidon (London), 1996.

Frampton Kenneth (ed), *Tadao Ando: Buildings Projects Writings*, Rizzoli (New York), 1984.

Fumihiko Maki 1986–1992, Space Design 01 (Tokyo), 1993.

Fumihiko Maki, JA: The Japan Architect, 16 (Tokyo), December 1994.

Fumihiko Maki: Buildings and Projects, Princeton Architectural Press (New York), 1997.

Futagawa Yukio (ed), *Tadao Ando 1972–1987, GA Architect 2*, ADA Edita (Tokyo), 1987.

— (ed), *Tadao Ando 1988–1993, GA Architect 12*, ADA Edita (Tokyo), 1993.

— (ed), *Shin Takamatsu, GA Architect 9* ADA Edita (Tokyo), 1990.

— (ed), *Tadao Ando, GA Document Extra 01* (Tokyo), 1995.

Itsuko Hasegawa, Architectural Monographs No. 31, Academy Editions (London), 1994.

Itsuko Hasegawa: Selected and Current Works, The Images Publishing Group (Mulgrave, Victoria), 1997.

Jodidio Philip, *Tadao Ando*, Taschen Verlag (Cologne), 1997.

Polledri Paolo (ed), *Shin Takamatsu* MoMA (San Francisco), and Rizzoli (New York), 1993.

Roulet Sophie and Sophie Soulie, *Toyo Ito: Architecture of the Ephemera* Editions du Moniteur (Paris), 1991.

Shin Takamatsu, JA Library 1 (Tokyo), 1993.

Toyo Ito, JA Library 2 (Tokyo), 1993.

Toyo Ito 1986–1995, EL Croquis 71 (Madrid), 1995.

Vitta Maurizio (ed), *Shin Takamatsu: Architecture and Nothingness*, L'Arca Edizioni (Milan), 1996.

Yoshio Taniguchi, JA, The Japan Architect (Tokyo), No 21, Spring 1996.

Contributors

Botond Bognar is Professor of
Architecture at the University of Illinois.
He is the author of numerous books
on Japanese architecture, including
*World Cities: Tokyo, The New Japanese
Architecture* and *The Japan Guide*,
and has contributed to numerous other
publications. His monograph on the
Japanese architect Togo Murano won
an AIA International Book Award in
1997.

Iain Borden is Senior Lecturer in
Architectural History and Sub-Dean of
the Faculty of the Built Environment at
The Bartlett, University College London.
He is co-editor of a number of books
including, *Architecture and the Sites
of History: Interpretations of Buildings
and Cities* and *Strangely Familiar:
Narratives of Architecture in the City*,
and is currently writing a theorized
history of skateboarding as a critical
urban practice.

Ilse Crawford is Consultant Editor of
Elle Decoration and Contributing Editor
of *The Observer*, and has recently been
appointed Vice President of Donna
Karan Homewares. She was
responsible for launching British *Elle
Decoration* in 1991 and was previously
Deputy Editor of *World of Interiors* and
Architects' Journal. She has also
written a book, *Sensual Home*.

Jayne Merkel is Editor of *Oculus*, an
independent monthly magazine
published by the AIA New York Chapter,
and contributes to many publications
including *Art in America, Artforum* and
Design Book Review. She is the author
of monographs on Michael Graves and
the firm of Pasanella + Klein Stolzman
+ Berg, and is currently working on a
book about the New York apartment
house.

Jeremy Myerson is a writer on design
and architecture, and Visiting Professor
of Contemporary Design at De Montfort
University, Leicester, UK. He was
formerly the editor of *Design Week*,
which he founded in 1986, and
Managing Editor of *World Architecture*.
He has written a number of books,
including *Gordon Russell: Designer of
Furniture, International Interiors*
volumes 5 and 6, and *Design
Renaissance*.

Antoine Predock is an internationally
renowned architect based in
Albuquerque, New Mexico. He gained
his reputation in the American West and
Southwest with works which connected
with their unique spiritual and historical
contexts, and has gone on to design
projects as far afield as Denmark,
Morocco and Los Angeles.

Picture credits

The publishers wish to thank all the
architect's offices, individuals, institutions and photographers that have
kindly supplied illustrations for this
book.

The pictures are numbered according
to page and their positions abbreviated
as l = left, r = right, c = centre,
b = bottom.

Cover

Interior photo of Mark Guard, House at
Deptford: John Edward Linden/Arcaid.
Photo reproduced with the kind
permission of William Richards
and Chris Mazeika. Designed by
Mark Vernon-Jones.

Introduction

2 Antoine Predock Architect, photo:
© Timothy Hursley; 7 Eurolounge;
8 Branson Coates, photo: Philip Vile
9 *Wallpaper*; 10 IKEA; 11 MoMA
Design Store, New York; 12 Graham
Mancha.

Statements

16(t) Branson Coates, photo: Philip
Vile; 16(b) Department of Trade and
Industry; 17 Wallpaper*; 18 Terence
Conran Ltd; 19 Ilse Crawford; 20 IKEA;
21(t) Richard Rogers Partnership,
photo: Eamonn O'Mahony; 21(b)
Richard Rogers Partnership.

Essays

23 Branson Coates, photo: Phil Sayer;
26 Richard Rogers Partnership, photo:
Eamonn O'Mahony; 27 Richard Rogers
Partnership, photo: R Davies;
28 Bernard Tschumi Architects, photo:
Peter Mauss/Esto; 29(t) Branson
Coates, photo: Phil Sayer; 29(b) ©
Grant Mudford; 33 Ilse Crawford; 37
Terence Conran Ltd; 38 & 39 © Peter
Cook/View; 40 & 41 Harper Mackay
Architects.

Britain

43 © Martin Charles; 46 Foster
Associates, photo: Dennis Gilbert;
47(t) © Martin Charles;
47(b) Nicholas Grimshaw & Partners,
photo: © Peter Cook/View; 48 ©
Richard Bryant/Arcaid; 49 © Peter
Cook/View; 52 & 53 Fin Architects &
Designers; 54 Future Systems; 56 &
57 Mark Guard Architects; 58 & 59(t)
© John Edward Linden/Arcaid; 59(b)
Mark Guard Architects; 60 & 61 Mark
Guard Architects; 62 & 63 © Richard
Bryant/Arcaid.

The USA

65 David A Loggie/Pierpont Morgan
Library; 70 Cooper Union Foundation
for Art and Science, New York, photo:
© Judith Turner; 71 Wexner Center for
the Arts, the Ohio State University,
Columbus, Ohio, photo: Kevin
Fitzsimmons; 72 photograph by David
Heald © SRGF, New York, 1997; 76 ©
Grant Mudford; 77 Michael Sorkin
Studio; 78, 79, 80 & 81(b) Richard
Gluckman Architects, photos: Lydia
Gould; 81(t) Richard Gluckman
Architects, photo: Tom Powel: 83
Richard Meier & Partners, photo: Scott
Frances; 84 Pasanella + Klein
Stolzman + Berg; 85(tl) & 85(bl)
Pasanella + Klein Stolzman + Berg;
85(br) © Jock Pottle/Esto; 86 & 87
photo: David Allison © 1997 The
Museum of Modern Art, New York;
88 & 89 Bernard Tschumi Architects,
photo: Peter Mauss/Esto; 90(l)
Voorsanger & Associates, photo: Carla
Breeze; 90(r) Voorsanger &
Associates; 91 Voorsanger &
Associates, photo: © Paul Warchol; 93,
94 & 95 Antoine Predock; 96, 97, 98 &
99 Antoine Predock Architect, photos:
© Timothy Hursley; 100, 101, 102 & 103
Wendell Burnette Architects.

Japan

All photographs © Botond Bognar.

Thanks to Matti Naar, Marketing
Manager of IKEA UK, for providing
the statement on page 20.